The Networking Diary

by
Nancy T. Nguyen, MBA

Foreword by D. Joel Whalen

Ms. Delray Beach,
Turn favorite body Bridel
Happy networking,
Nancy :)

The Networking Diary
by Nancy T. Nguyen, MBA

Published through Publishing Unleashed
www.publishingunleashed.com

Interior Book Design by Integrative Ink
www.integrativeink.com

ISBN-13: 978-1-4701-1256-1
ISBN-10: 1-4701-1256-6

Note:
The author has tried to recreate events, locales, and conversations from memory. In order to maintain the anonymity of the parties involved, the names of certain individuals and places have been changed, along with identifying characteristics and details, such as physical properties, occupations, and places of residence.

CONTENTS

ACKNOWLEDGMENTS

My parents arrived in Raleigh, NC with a little red plaid suitcase and me. Families from St. Raphael's Church helped my immigrant family find our first apartment, job, and baby crib. I thank all the people who never judged me for how little I had but instead appreciated me for how much I wanted to give.

This book could not have been written without the help of D. Joel Whalen, Ph.D., who not only served as my professor at DePaul University Kellstadt Graduate School of Business but who also encouraged and challenged me throughout my academic program. DePaul's faculty members, friends, and fellow entrepreneurs have encouraged me to proceed fearlessly. I thank the DePaul MBA Association, Alpha Kappa Psi's Tau Chi chapter, and the Ms./Mrs. Corporate America Pageant for giving me the opportunity to serve your organizations.

To all the friends I made while living in Chicago, you continue to inspire me. To all my friends in Raleigh, thank you for cultivating my Southern values and for allowing me to be a Wolfpack. To all my friends worldwide, I think of you often and thank you for sharing your time with me. To all of my hair clients worldwide, thank you for sharing your stories with me. To a special client, Tanya Stockton, and her business colleague, Maryellen Smith, thank you for guiding me through the publishing process, never accepting less than my best efforts. To all of my friends and colleagues at corporate, The Chicago White Sox, The City of Chicago's DHR, and Sweet T Salon, thank you for providing me with unique conversations. To every single person who's shared time to read this book or network with me—thank you.

FOREWORD

You're about to shave years off the time it would take you to become an expert networker. You're going on an adventure in networking with a young woman that will change your life.

Nancy T. Nguyen (pronounced *Win* like the winner she is) leads a life of international travel, behind the scenes work with a major league baseball team, while driving wild success and revenue growth for her entrepreneurial company and reigning as Ms. Corporate America. Nancy takes you on that journey with her. I'm amazed to realize that she's still in her 20s.

You'll learn the *Seven Network Diary Principles*. You'll learn vicariously by reading her e-mail threads and hearing her recounted conversations as she builds and manages relationships with an ego-bloated publisher, a brilliant HR consultant, and a control-freak association manager. After each story in her diary, you'll get Nancy's candid analysis of what really happened as she networked with that particular person. Plus, you'll get networking rules for success and check lists that help you navigate around networking's alligator pits.

You'll be amazed as you see Nancy networking with an emergency room X-ray technician minutes after she was hit and run by an SUV. Even while enduring searing pain from a broken shoulder, Nancy networks. Why such fierce dedication to networking? Is Nancy T. Nguyen driven by other-worldly forces? Hardly. She knows the secret to happiness and success in life: Networking. It's not something you just turn off and on. Once you get in the networking flow, it builds its own self-sustaining momentum.

To know Nancy is to rejoice in her open-hearted approach to life. She is dedicated to the service of others. She embodies what we at DePaul University call *Personalism*: Every individual counts. We work to raise-up people to help them get more from their lives. Thus, our lives are enriched. That is the essence of the Nancy T. Nguyen approach to networking.

Nancy is going to show you how networking is:

- finding ways to give to others before you get from them
- a constant process; a long-term experience
- about building trust before you try to give

Reading Nancy's diary will open your eyes. Networking may not be what you think it is. Just the other night after class an exceptionally bright DePaul MBA Candidate, an executive with a big-three financial firm, brought his problems with networking to me. "I go to networking events," he complained, "but, I don't know what I should be wanting to get out of them. How do I know what to expect to get?"

Here's what I told that young man:

Networking is not an event. It's the way you live your life. Networking is how we use social media and face-to-face events to expand our social world. To get the best benefits you must be an active participant of an organization for three to five years. Until that time, you're a stranger to most members—the new guy. Now, I'm not saying that you'll not benefit sooner, you will. **The maximum benefits take longer.**

Networking is not about getting, it's about giving. You network to find people you can help and to find ways to share your assets and contacts with them. When you give to someone else first, you set up a savings account of good favors with that person. When you help someone, they have a deep need, a compulsion, to help you back. Want a good book? Read *Influence* by Robert Cialdini. He'll show you how to use powerful psychological techniques to get what you want by helping others. Look for his discovery: *Reciprocation.*

Networking is not LinkedIn or a meeting in a hotel ballroom. Networking happens whenever two people meet to find ways to help each other. Nancy takes advantage of her diminutive 4'10" stature by volunteering to take the middle seat on airplanes. "That way I get to meet a new person on my left and my right." Of course, that may not work for you, but you get what she means.

Successful politicians and top sales people know how to network. So do Hollywood agents, sports agents, and every minister, rabbi, mullah, priest, and yogi who leads a following. And, after reading *The Networking Diary*, so will you.

I'll be looking forward to seeing how I can help you. My first bit of help for you is to encourage you to read, enjoy, and apply the principles found in *The Networking Diary*.

Best regards from America's Favorite City,
—D. Joel Whalen

Associate Professor of Marketing
Kellstadt Graduate School of Business
Academic Director, Center for Sales Leadership
Creator, Breakthrough Communication Method
DePaul University, Chicago
Author: *I See What You Mean* and
Professional communication Toolkit, Sage Publications

PREFACE

HOW THIS BOOK IS WRITTEN—
AND WHY

The Networking Diary provides seven principles that will help you take the fear out of networking. The process of networking is not a science—it is an art. Therefore, this is *not* a "How to" book; instead, it is a compilation of true networking experiences.

Upon moving from Raleigh, NC to Chicago, IL, then back, I was connected to about 200 personal and professional contacts online. In one year, I increased my network to over 3,000 personal contacts; however, networking is not a popularity contest, nor is it solely used to get what *you* want.

To set you at ease and prove to you that the process is not as complex as you may believe, I am going to share real networking. Instead of simply presenting seven principles and telling you how to network, I am going to share real networking stories that demonstrate networking in action. Like many of my childhood friends, and probably like you, I had a locked diary where I recorded events from my days. I am "opening the lock" for you to see the awkward side of business networking—the interactions that no one ever talks about. I made a lot of mistakes, but you don't have to!

As a 4'10" petite Asian gal, I could blend in with a room of 4th graders. I have had to walk into networking events solo and try to make meaningful business connections.

When I've networked with other men during lunch, they are sometimes unsure of whether they should pull out my chair. The stories that I will share with you in *The Networking Diary* fundamentally relate to feeling confident in yourself and projecting an air of professionalism regardless of what others might assume about you based upon your gender or overall appearance. You will also see how networking can be used to connect people of different generations, cultures, and professional positions.

NETWORKING DOES NOT REQUIRE A COLLEGE DEGREE, GREAT LOOKS, OR A HIGH IQ

The great thing about business networking is that you build long-term relationships with colleagues, vendors, and clients. I stress the term "long-term relationship" and do not want to misconstrue networking to be a sales plan. Business networking does not require a college degree, great looks, or a high IQ.

Unlike some of my college friends, I did not have wealthy parents, a high GPA, or business mentors. I graduated from North Carolina State University with a meager 2.9 GPA. After my undergraduate studies, I applied to business school at local universities in my hometown and didn't get accepted.

I didn't have the grades or the background, but I did have the desire to learn how to create meaningful connections in business communities. My parents never finished high school; in fact, my dad never finished middle school. Through networking, each of my parents built a loyal clientele for their businesses from the ground up.

I have often wondered, *"Why is it that so many people land jobs easily while others can't even get an initial inter-*

view? Why do some employees make it to the top of an orga-nization while others spend years in the same cubicle? Why do straight-A students sometimes work for college dropouts? Why do some small business owners experience sales growth while others go bankrupt during a volatile economy?" The answer to these questions is "networking" since it involves synergetic relationships. People form networks for various purposes. Networking can be helpful as you begin your new career or move to a new city.

After undergraduate school and moving to Chicago with nothing but two suitcases, I landed my first corporate job within four weeks. Thanks to online resume posting sites, a recruiter for a large beauty company found me and inter-viewed me at a coffee shop. During my time spent there as a manager, I faced numerous challenges. The position had been vacant for several months, so I worked hard to reverse a 19% decrease in service revenue and develop a cohesive team.

My enthusiasm towards networking and can-do atti-tude helped me approach these challenges. Within my first three months of joining the company, I exceeded my first corporate goal by 103.8% and my second by 16.0%. I also decreased employee turnover by 43%—and by the end of the fiscal year. The sales of my team increased by 15.1%, and I met my staffing goals. My team and I were proud to be #3 in the company of 202 locations nationwide. Being a part of this large corporation taught me to network with senior executives, clients, and outside partners.

An MBA Is Not a Prerequisite to Networking

I thought that an MBA was a prerequisite to holding a higher management job within a company so I chose to go back to school. While working toward my MBA, I landed an HR job at the Chicago White Sox by applying for it on Craigslist.com. After two baseball seasons, I applied online to work for the Commissioner of Human Resources for the City of Chicago. I thought, *If I work really hard, I will move up in the department.* While I was partly correct, I learned through my personal experiences, blue-collar parents, and business mentors that networking is a must in the business world. Networking can be as valuable as a college degree and doing everything your boss tells you to do (sometimes more so!).

Since people have different personalities, I cannot tell you specifically how you should network. However, I want to share with you seven principles I use that have helped me build meaningful business relationships while networking. These principles include making sure that your networking relationships are mutually beneficial, defining your networking goal, being properly prepared to connect with others, valuing your contact's time, following up with your contacts, maintaining a professional demeanor, and learning to take advantage of the networking opportunities that may present themselves to you in your day-to-day life.

It is not my interest to introduce another "How to" book into the market, but to share how I have successfully applied the seven principles listed above to every networking opportunity presented. Using the Internet, my MBA, and the opportunities presented in the many unique positions I have held, I have gathered networking experiences, which are presented in the diary entries that follow. You will see the good, the bad, and the ugly side of *real* networking opportunities. It is my hope that you will also gain the confidence necessary to take the fear out of networking by applying my seven proven principles.

FOR YOUR PERSONAL NETWORKING OPPORTUNITIES

With the unemployment rate rising, it is essential to add networking to your agenda. As a small business owner, I spend 80% of my time working on the business and networking and 20% *in* the business! Basically, 80% of my time is spent networking and creating new strategies to bring in clients. The remaining 20% is spent on completing tasks that my employees do.

I've done pretty well for myself, and I feel that everyone can benefit from learning my techniques. Within one year of purchasing my first hair salon in Raleigh, NC, we experienced between a 54%-88% sales growth in one year. We also increased our staff by 150% in a bad economy. How? Networking. My proven techniques work in any business or industry in any economic climate.

Right now, I am sitting at RDU Airport and have already conversed with five people who genuinely want to come to my hair salon. In fact, one lady said, "I have to tell my sister about you!" Networking opportunities are everywhere! My focus is on helping you build your business, build your brand, and create more opportunities for yourself.

Many of the principles listed in *The Networking Diary* have been inspired by Dale Carnegie's classic, *How to Win Friends and Influence People.* Modern day issues are faced again and again in the world of networking: the generation gap, getting into the "Boys' Club," gender differences and equality, cultural changes, dirty politics, ethics, lack of time, and technological advances are only a few. Each chapter covers a modern-day issue related to one of the seven principles, followed by an actual diary entry showing that principle in action. Additional references are available for anyone wanting to enhance their networking ability no matter where they are in their career!

PART I

WHY SHOULD YOU NETWORK?

WHY TAKE THE TIME TO MAKE VALUABLE CONNECTIONS?

According to statistics on how Americans find employment, 35% find jobs through a friend, relative, or other associate. Studies have found that 65% of people who are employed found a job that was never publicly advertised. According to Robert Half Management Resources, 70% to 80% of all corporate positions are acquired through personal and professional connections. Some people can naturally develop a plan and a network of contacts to find ways to enhance their careers; however, I have observed that for most people, networking is unnatural.

It is a goal of mine to train my employees to be master networkers. When I first purchased a beauty salon and rebranded it, I had only one employee. Within one year, I hired 10 employees and grew the business by 54% during a bad economy. I did it by networking. I also shared networking stories with my employees every day. They began to implement principles shared in this book to build long-lasting relationships with their clientele, increase sales, and to grow our company's brand.

There are many resources on the Internet, at career fairs, and with personal and business contacts. Everyone has someone who knows someone who has a job vacancy, resource, or advice that can be purposeful. However, it can often become time-consuming, frightening, or confusing to network.

My clients share stories about losing their jobs, not liking their current jobs, and needing to find additional jobs. I have shared *The Networking Diary* principles with hundreds of clients. It makes my heart sing when I hear the stories of my clients' successful networking.

WHAT IS NETWORKING?

During my reign as Ms. Corporate America, I presented to students at our county's Youth Educated and Succeeding (Y.E.S.) meeting. I asked the students, ages 16-21, "What is networking?" After a few minutes, a young lady raised her hand and said, "It's connecting with others."

This was an excellent answer! Business networking refers to the art of creating professional opportunities by coming in contact with like-minded men and women of various backgrounds and developing mutually beneficial relationships with them. Men and women can exchange ideas and referrals, obtain specialized information, and create new career opportunities.

WHAT KIND OF NETWORKING DO YOU NEED?

There are two primary ways I have cultivated my network. My favorite way to network takes place in person. I actually enjoy sitting in the middle seat on a plane because I have the opportunity to meet someone to my left and right, if they are sociable. As a member of many local business groups, I attend meetings where other professionals share their knowledge and resources, leading to more lasting relationships.

My second business networking method is conducted over the Internet using LinkedIn, e-mail, Facebook, and Twitter. This allows us to expand our community without ever leaving the comfort of our home offices. The advantage of this approach is that it is less time consuming, and I can conduct rapid research on my person of contact. I can also virtually communicate with members in national professional associations.

Is in-person networking or online social networking better? With limited time, online social networking works best. It is also better for maintaining contact and discussing a variety of topics with large groups of people. You can also expand your relationships beyond where time and travel costs allow with traditional face-to-face networking. However, online social networking will never replace face-to-face networking. To accelerate your networking success, it is important to balance meaningful conversations in person and to connect with people on the Internet.

PART II

SEVEN NETWORKING DIARY PRINCIPLES

Networking Diary Principle 1:
It Is Not All about You

Networking Diary Principle 2:
Define Your Networking Goal

Networking Diary Principle 3:
You've Connected, Now Be Prepared

Networking Diary Principle 4:
Value Your Contact's Time

Networking Diary Principle 5:
Follow Up or Forget It

Networking Diary Principle 6:
Always Be Professional

Networking Diary Principle 7:
Networking Is Everywhere

NETWORKING DIARY PRINCIPLE #1

IT IS NOT ALL ABOUT YOU

We all need a daily check up from the neck up to avoid stinkin' thinkin' which ultimately leads to hardening of the attitudes. –Zig Ziglar

Ready, Set, Network! You understand the importance of networking, but what makes networking important to *you*? Is it to find a new job? It is to move up in your company? Is it to pitch your new idea? Is it to get advice? Is it to sell your service or product? All of these questions are focused on you.

After dozens of late night networking events and following up with people I meet, I fill up binders and shoeboxes with business cards. Sales people follow up with me and then lose touch. What a waste of time to go to all these networking events, come home with tons of business cards, and not see most of these people again! The daunting networking goal to grab as many cards as you can does not build authentic relationships. I get tired of investing time and money networking this way.

Successful networking is not all about you. One secret to successful networking is being able to help *others* solve their problems *while* keeping your intentions in mind. Have you ever met someone, and all they talk about is themselves? Then they enjoy talking to you because they are able to talk about themselves. Here is an example of that kind of networker.

Networking Diary Entry
November 12

Today, my mentor sent me an e-mail with the subject line, "I Thought of You Last Night." The e-mail read, *"I thought of you last night when I was out at a networking event. An insurance agent talked on and on about himself and his business, then gave me his card and wrote on the back: Call me. Totally not cool! Just thought you'd be amused. I'm sure you've seen it all! Bye for now, Marcie."*

DIARY ENTRY LEARNING LESSONS

Before you network, set your attitude to focus on the person with whom you are networking instead of just yourself. Change your mind about what you're networking for. Instead of passing out business cards as quickly as possible and making the initial contact with Marcie all about himself, the insurance man needed to let Marcie talk about herself, too.

1. Remember, it's not all about you. The insurance agent never asked Marcie anything about herself—why she was there, or if he could help her with anything. He made the conversation all about himself and ended with giving a card that Marcie did not need.

2. Have a mutually beneficial purpose that is not all about you. His purpose during this networking

event was to sell insurance. People buy relation-ships, not businesses. By making a quick sales pitch to Marcie, he missed opportunities to find out who Marcie is and what her needs are.

3. Intentional, strategic networking trumps random handing business card networking.

EXERCISE

Before you hand out your business card, ask yourself the following questions:

1. Is there a purpose for me in reaching out to this person?

2. Would this connection be mutually beneficial?

Take the time to think about the underlying purpose of the connection before you reach out to someone.

NETWORKING DIARY PRINCIPLE 2

DEFINE YOUR NETWORKING GOAL

To reach a port, we must sail—Sail, not tie at anchor—Sail, not drift. –Franklin Roosevelt

At some point in your career, you have probably entered a large, crowded room of unfamiliar business professionals dressed in suits who have given you business cards and asked to "do lunch." Sometimes, I walk away from events with over a dozen business cards to pick through to see who would be interested in:

- career opportunities
- consulting offers
- new ventures
- expertise requests
- business deals
- getting back in touch

I go to networking events, but with the goal of truly getting to know people and getting people to know me. This networking goal takes time and commitment. In other words, building trust takes time and commitment. Once I saw a guy at the airport exchange cards with another guy and say, "Hey man, I'll take you up on that beer you mentioned." Although I did not hear the man's goal in this networking interaction, I saw that the two of them had created a bond with each other in a short period of time. Building friendships boosts credibility over time in business.

Here is a story about a young gentleman who reached out to me online with his networking goal. This example also demonstrates the first principle in action.

Networking Diary Entry
October 11

LinkedIn: Blake Paisley has indicated you are a Classmate at North Carolina State University

Nancy,

I am a fellow NC State graduate and it appears that we are both in the business of meeting people. I am interested in meeting more alumni in the area. I would like to add you to my professional network and have an opportunity to introduce myself.

Thank you,
Blake Paisley

How exciting to have a fellow alumni from my alma mater in Raleigh, NC want to connect with me in Chicago, IL! I called Blake to "do lunch" and find out more about his current goals.

October 11
Re: Confirming for 10/13 12:35 pm Lunch at Café

Blake,

I hope that you have had a wonderful week-end. I am confirming our lunch on October 13 at 12:35 pm. The Café is at State and Washington. Reach my cell if you need to call/text me.

Thank you,
Nancy

 October 11
Re: Confirming for 10/13 12:35 pm Lunch at Café

Nancy,

That sounds great, I will see you then.

Blake Paisley

We entered the café ten minutes before our confirmed time and were greeted by my friends who work there. I love networking at this place. The tables have white paper table covers (where I sometimes write down ideas while meeting with people), the servers know your name, and the afford-able lunch specials are delightful. Usually the bill is split in half at the end of the meeting. I normally order something in the same price range as my guest. Blake ordered a bowl of squash soup and half of a sandwich, and I did the same. It was nice to meet someone from NC State University in the Chicago area.

At that time, I was working for a Commissioner at the City of Chicago, and Blake was a financial advisor. More than two-dozen financial advisors contacted me that year. Ha! I am not sure why, because with tons of school loans, I did not have any money to advise with.

During lunch, Blake asked me if I knew certain names. I eagerly said, "Yes" and shared why I knew the particular name he brought up. "She's great! I did her hair for her wedding" and "He's in my MBA Association, and we've been on a camping trip," were some of my responses. I grew more and more excited about all the names he'd mentioned because I assumed he knew the same people.

At the end of the list of names, Blake asked, "Can I get an introduction to these people?" I couldn't believe it! All this time, I thought that he personally knew all the people I knew. However, I quickly realized that he'd simply copied a list of names from my LinkedIn profile.

My first thought was, *It took* years *to build relationships with these people, and you want me to hand off my friends to you to capitalize on?!*

The response that came out of my mouth was, "How about you come to our MBA Association's Third Thursday event, and I will introduce you to the majority of the people you have on your list? There is also a class that you can attend with me to meet other entrepreneurs. I can give you an introduction that way, too."

I realized that he probably thought that by being from the same town and same school, I would connect him to all of the people on the list that he'd printed. People ask to be connected to certain people here and there, but I have never met anyone who has shown me a printed list of names. I was disappointed that Blake was focused solely on his Return on Networking (R.O.N.) more so than on bringing value to our meeting.

To help Blake connect to my contacts, I invited him to networking events these people regularly attend and to one of my classes to meet with people face-to-face. It would not be a problem to introduce him to everyone on the list because I love connecting people. But I wanted to see whether he was willing to take initiative to show up to the events to meet most of the people he was targeting.

October 13
Re: Thank you

Blake,

Thank you for lunch at the café today. It was a pleasure to meet you. Let me know when you are able to come to any Thursday event or class. You can also register at www.DePaulMBA.org for all future updates.

Warmest,
Nancy

October 13
Re: Thank you

Nancy,

It was my pleasure, and I enjoyed meeting you as well. Thank you for the help with the introductions to people that you know. I will follow up with the introduction email that we discussed. I will be at the event on Thursday night, but not the class. I am looking forward to seeing you on Thursday, have a great day!

Regards,
Blake Paisley

During a Thursday networking event with the DePaul MBA Association, Blake sent me a text indicating that he would not be able to attend. He missed opportunities to meet most of the people he'd mentioned during our lunch meeting. Networking is like a part-time job. You have to put work into it. In this case, all Blake had to do was show up to the event, and he had me as an advocate to make introductions.

October 17
Re: Follow Up

Nancy,

I hope that you had a great time last night, and I am sorry that I was not able to make it out.

I woke up feeling awful and thought that I might feel better throughout the day, however that never happened. I am looking forward to making another event, so please let me know more about the class that you attend on Thursdays.

I really enjoyed having lunch with you. You are an energetic and exciting person to be around. I appreciate your help with introductions to some of your contacts. What I have found to be the best approach is to shoot them a quick email to let them know that I will be reaching out, so that I do not catch them off guard. I have attached a short introduction that you can use. Below are the people that we discussed on Tuesday:

[Here he attached a list of the names again.]

I would like to start reaching out to them on Thursday. Please let me know if you need more time to send out the email. Also if you could let me know what the best number to reach them at would be. Thank you again for your help, and have a great weekend. Let's touch base early part of next week.

———

Here is the attached letter that he expected ME to e-mail the list of names he'd extracted from my LinkedIn profile:

Hello,

This is just a note to introduce Blake Paisley, who will be getting in touch with you soon.

Blake runs a financial services practice in Chicago, and has shared with me some ideas in the risk management and financial areas that have been quite helpful.

Neither Blake nor I are assuming that you would be in the market for his services, however, I felt very positive about our meeting, and thought you might benefit from a conversation with him as well.

Probably, like me, you are not eager to talk to another person in this business, but in this case it might be well to make an exception.
Best,
Blake Paisley

This guy was obviously trying to promote his services to people I personally knew. How rude of him to comb through my LinkedIn profile for more than twenty names, give me a list, and then ask me to connect him to them just because we have the same alma mater! Some of the people on the list are CEOs who would kill me if I gave a financial advisor their contact information.

Blake had a clear networking goal of connecting to my list of personal contacts for his financial services. I would try to help, but Bret needed to attend events and get in-person introductions.

October 17
Re: Follow Up

Blake,

Thank you for your e-mail. I am swamped this weekend, but I will reach out to people on this list. Some may be open to connecting to new people. Honestly, the others would not be as open to connecting due to their current situations. Give me some time to talk to people in person first. However, the best thing for you to do is attend some of our MBA networking groups.

Thank you,
Nancy

Blake never showed up to any networking events to meet even half the people on the list he'd created. He sent an e-mail eight months later sharing a new goal given to him by his bosses.

 June 2
Re: Introduction

Nancy,

I hope you are doing well. It has been a while since we spoke. I hope your travels have been going well. Our Director of Recruiting, Mary Monier, will be contacting you in the next few days or so. She asked me for some help identifying individuals that I thought were real intelligent, hard working, great all around people. Our organization is always looking to grow substantially, and I thought of you. I am not assuming you are unhappy with your current job, but I know you are always open to hearing about more opportunities. If you aren't interested at this point, you may know of someone else. Let me know if you are not open to spending 60 seconds on the phone with her and I'll pass this along to her.

All the best,
Blake Paisley

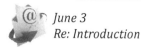

June 3
Re: Introduction

Dear Blake,

Thank you for your e-mail. It is wonderful to hear from you.
Hopefully, your travels have gone well, too.
I am currently in Raleigh, NC and traveling. E-mail is best for me because my voicemail rarely gets checked. Please feel free to pass on my information.

Sincerely,
Nancy

Blake was a bright young financial advisor. He also seemed like he'd be a good friend to have. His goals were clear in his e-mails; however, every time he contacted me, he sent a sales script that had probably been coached to him.

When I first moved to Chicago, my first job was door-to-door sales. It was not a fun job, but the President of the company taught us effective sales scripts to use. I can now identify when sales people use "sales tricks" to stroke my ego to try and sell me something.

After eight months, Blake said, "I hope you are doing well." First of all, I am sure that he did not genuinely care. Second of all, never start an e-mail off with "I" or "my."

"It has been a while since we spoke," Blake adds. Yes, it had, and the only time he wanted to speak was when his boss sent him out to sell or recruit.

Then he tops off the e-mail with an ego booster. "Our Director of Recruiting...asked me for help identifying individuals that I thought were real *intelligent, hardworking, great all around people.* I am not assuming you are unhappy with your current job." Blake wanted to sell his services to me without building a relationship, *and* he wanted to recruit me to be a salesperson like him. He would now send his Director of Recruiting to try and close a deal with me.

 June 24
Re: Financial Group

Hi Nancy

Blake Paisley had passed along your information to me as someone who might be open-minded to discuss their career and really just see what else is out there. He did not infer that you are looking for a change, but thought highly enough of you to pass along your information to me as someone who would be open-minded. He mentioned you were travelling a lot and thought to give you a few weeks to catch up and then email you. Please contact me at your earliest convenience as I would love to sit down with you and have a conversation about your career aspirations and goals. Have a nice evening.

Mary Monier

June 30
Re: Thank you for your message

Dear Mary,

Hello and thank you for your recent phone call. I was in Atlanta when I received your message. Currently, I am working on my companies and new fashion line. This limits my time to meet. However, please feel free to let me know what you are recruiting for.

Sincerely,
Nancy

June 30
Re: Thank you for your message

Hi Nancy-

Thank you for following up. I hope the rest of your travels go smoothly. I am looking to meet with hardworking individuals that are entrepreneurial, money driven, like to help others, and have a good head on their shoulders. That's how your name came up in conversation with Blake. I have attached a job description if that helps. The first step would really be getting to know one another though. Let me know what you're thinking and if you would be open minded to sitting down and having a conversation about where your future career path is leading you. Thanks Nancy and have a safe holiday weekend.

July 6
Re: Thank you for your message

Dear Mary,

At this time, I am swamped with my start up and my regular job. However, I can schedule a short conference call if that works for you.

Thank you,
Nancy

It was no surprise that I never heard from Blake or Mary again.

DIARY ENTRY LEARNING LESSONS

1. Your networking goal should not be about pushing your agenda on others. Blake connected with me on LinkedIn to have easy access to my friends, mentors, and other connections. I offered him a chance to meet people face-to-face and he never showed up. Then eight months later, he tried to recruit me into his firm as a sales person by giving me sales pitches his bosses taught him. He had eight months to create a long-term relationship and failed to do so.

2. The primary networking goal you should have is to build relationships for the long haul. Someone once said, More business happens outside of busi-

ness. Networking outside of the boardroom, stuffy business suits, and business meetings at cafés helps build long-term relationships.

3. It takes hard work and commitment to build these long-term relationships. However, if you make this your primary goal for networking, you will have authentic advocates. You want to be known as an ethical, reliable, and resourceful person. Since completing my MBA, I still remain in contact with former classmates, attend their weddings, and am now waiting for new baby announcements. As a salon owner, I have watched football games with clients, attended funerals, and know about their children's graduations. Setting your goal to building long-term relationships on trust is valuable while networking.

EXERCISE

Long-term relationships are simply built on trust. I can trust the people in my network to be on time when we meet. They can trust me to refer them to the right resources when they need help. You might not want a long-term relationship with everyone in your network, but it does not mean you cannot stay connected online, through affiliations, or with a simple phone call every now and then.

1. Think about the people you trust and like. Continue to cultivate a long-term relationship with them. Networking does not always have to be centered on

current business goals. Remember, more business happens outside of business.

2. The next time you meet someone with whom you would like to create a long-term relationship, ask what their current goals are and how you can help them. Then follow up by helping them connect to people and resources you trust.

NETWORKING DIARY PRINCIPLE 3

YOU'VE CONNECTED, NOW BE PREPARED

Before anything else, preparation is the key to success. –Alexander Graham Bell

You are smart. You would not go into a job interview without researching the company for whom you want to work. This practice should be applied to networking as well. Have you ever gone to a networking event and spotted someone who seemed completely out of place? I have been that person and hated the awkwardness. The difference between my early awkward networking days and today is in the preparation. In this chapter, I am going to share with you a story about how a mentor, who is the CEO of one of the top companies in Illinois, introduced me to his friend to help me with this book. His friend is a Hollywood actor, successful author, and a well-known businessman.

Prior to meeting with Dick, my mentor's friend, I set some goals, thought about my introduction, and researched his background through sources like his LinkedIn profile. It is hard work to connect with a high-level businessman in the first place, and I quickly learned that it is even harder work once you have connected with him!

Networking Diary Entry
February 12

Tim spoke to our business Capstone class last summer about his company. I ran into him by the elevators at DePaul University's downtown Chicago campus a few months later, and we briefly spoke. In the beginning of the year, the secretary for the Chicago Commissioner for whom I was interning gave me the latest *Crain's Chicago* magazine. Of the four interns, I was the only business student. When the mail arrived, the secretary gave me all business-related magazines. The articles made the temporary "cubicle life" more bearable. Tim's name appeared in *Crain's* because he was interviewed for an article about the New Year's resolutions of entrepreneurs.

I highlighted his quote, sent him a "Congratulations" e-mail for appearing in *Crain's*, and met with him a couple of weeks later to learn more about his business. His daughter and I are the same age and in the same business school. Sometimes mentors who are much older treat you like their own children. During our meeting, I shared with Tim ideas for this book, and he loved it. He even contributed, "When I network with women, I never know if I am supposed to pull the chair out for them." I chuckled and told him, "No, because it is not a date. You treat women you are networking with like any professional man or woman. You wouldn't pull out the chair for a man, so that goes for women, too, when it comes to business networking."

After our lunch conversation full of entrepreneurial ideas, Tim connected me through e-mail to his friend Dick, who was already an accomplished author.

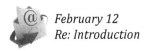

February 12
Re: Introduction

Good afternoon Nancy and Dick. Please consider this an introduction and invitation to communicate directly.

I met Nancy last summer when I was a guest presenter for Dr. Thompson's MBA class.

We have stayed in touch and seen each other when I was downtown at DePaul's campus.

Nancy is brilliant, and has many brilliant ideas. She is a true serial entrepreneur waiting to launch. Her ideas are well thought out. She is personable, connected and hard working.

She discussed an idea for a book that I thought was very interesting. I immediately thought of Dick and thought you two should meet over coffee and share ideas. Nancy can be reached via e-mail.

Dick is equally brilliant. He is a former Hollywood actor who left the lifestyle to return to his Midwest roots and develop his other qualities. Dick is a Principal with the Rough Paper Company. He has co-authored 5 books. Nancy had lunch Friday with us. During lunch, Edward mentioned how he took the Spanish version of one of your books home for his 13-year-old daughter to read. She couldn't put it down. She speaks and reads English better than Spanish.

I think you two will have a great connection—who knows where it can lead. You are both very special.

Tim

February 12
Re: Introduction

Tim,

Thank you so much for this introduction!
Nancy, I'd be happy to schedule a time to talk.
Please let me know your availability.

Best always,
Dick

February 12
Re: To schedule a call with you on 2/21, 2/23,
2/24, or 2/25.

Dear Dick,

Thank you for taking the time out of your busy day to reply. If your schedule permits, a call on 2/21, 2/23, 2/24, or 2/25 can work.

I truly look forward to hearing your expert opinion about a project that highlights the contributions of first generation immigrants.

Your time is very important, and I am more than happy to work around your schedule. Once we select a date, I will call you at the most convenient number.

Nancy

February 14
Re: To schedule a call with you on 2/21, 2/23,
2/24, or 2/25.

Thank you Nancy,

Linda Cohen handles my schedule and she'll be happy to set up a time with you that works for both of us.
I'll be looking forward to it.

Best always,
Dick

February 14
Re: To schedule a call with you on 2/21, 2/23,
2/24, or 2/25.

Dear Dick,

Perfect. Thank you for directing me to Linda. Ms. Cohen and I will take it from here.
I am thrilled connecting with you. Have a wonderful day.

Sincerely,
Nancy

February 15
Re: Phone Call - Dick

Good afternoon, Ms. Nguyen,

I received a note from Dick that you would like to schedule a phone call with him.

He has availability on 2/23, in the morning (9amCST-11amCST). If you are available during that period of time, please let me know when and I will block off a 30-minute phone call in his calendar. Also, please include the best phone number to reach you at that time.

If this time does not work for you, please feel free to send me several that do so that I may coordinate.

Best,
Linda

February 15
Re: Phone Call - Dick

Good afternoon, Ms. Linda,

Thank you for your lightning-fast response. It is truly appreciated. Are there any days for 30 minutes during these times: 7-9 a.m., 12-2 p.m., 6-10 p.m.? For 2/16, 2/21, 2/23, 2/24, 3/2, 3/3?

Sincerely,
Nancy

February 15
Re: Phone Call - Dick

Yes! It looks as though I could squeeze you in on Tuesday, 2/23, at 12pm CST. Does this work for you?

Linda Cohen

 February 15
Re: Confirmed Tuesday, 2/23, at 12pmCST Phone Call - Dick

Linda,

This is amazing. My luckiest number in the world is "23" and the call will be on 2/23.

It is going to be a great call. E-mail me if anything changes. I am more than happy to accommodate.

Thank you for this opportunity,
Nancy

February 15
Re: Confirmation - Phone Call 2/23

Nancy,

There is no doubt everything happens for a reason. :)
A phone call is confirmed for Tuesday, 2/23, at 12pmCST. Dick will call you.
Please let me know if your schedule changes!

Best,
Linda

February 15
Re: Confirmation - Phone Call 2/23

Linda,

For sure :). It is a pleasure to meet you here. I am sure that I will get to meet you in person sometime.
I am utterly excited. In the meantime, you will find in the links below how passionate I am about helping young professional who came from nothing like me go to college and make something of themselves.

Enjoy the fun surprises,
Nancy

February 15
Re: Confirmation - Phone Call 2/23

Nancy,

A very noble passion, indeed. I look forward to hearing about the call!

Best,
Linda

 February 23
Re: Confirmation - Phone Call 2/23 12:00 pm CST

Dear Linda,

As long as no emergencies happen here in my office at City Hall. I will be ready at 12:00 p.m. for Dick at 312-498-7648. If anything happens, I will e-mail you asap.

Thank you,
Nancy

February 23
Re: Confirmation - Phone Call 2/23 12:00 pm CST

Nancy,

Excellent. Of course, you can't control emergencies so just let me know if something comes up! Otherwise, Dick will be calling!

Best,
Linda

February 23
Re: Thank you

Dear Linda,

Thank you so much for setting up the call. Dick is such a joy.
Is there an address where I can send him a hand-written note?

Sincerely,
Nancy

February 23
Re: Thank you

Certainly.

Linda

 February 23
Re: Thank you

You are awesome. Thank you.

Nancy

During the phone conversation between Dick and me, I stood underneath a staircase on a different floor of the building at my job in order to keep the conversation private.

Here is the basic networking formula I follow in a phone call with a new connection:

1. Thank the person for his or her time, remind him or her how you connected, and review the time that the conversation will end.

2. Ask the opening question for the connection to answer.

3. Listen for ways to help the person talking.

4. Share current goals applicable to the new contact.

5. Listen for any possible new resources/information the contact may have, and try to give the contact resources/information.

6. Thank the contact for his or her time. If and ONLY if there is a MUTUALLY beneficial relationship, ask if you can meet in the future.

Using this formula, these were the opening statements in our 30-minute conversation:

1. *Thank you, Dick, for your time. It is nice of Tim to connect us. You have approximately 30 minutes for this call, correct?*

2. *I read that you have an extensive background in publishing. Can you share any advice for an aspiring writer?*

3. *Your bilingual English/Spanish book seems very good. I would love to help you promote it because I am part of many Hispanic business groups.*

4. *The Networking Diary is a book that might work well for your company. I would love the chance to show you the drafts completed so far and see if it would match the needs of your company.*

5. *Let me know how I can help you reach out to more Hispanic communities, porque hablo Español tambien.*

6. *Thank you so much for sharing your time today. May I please reach out to you for lunch one day in a few weeks?*

Dick immediately mailed me a copy of his English/Spanish book. It took some time before Dick and I reconnected, but in the meantime, I thanked Tim for connecting us.

At this time, I was juggling two graduate classes at DePaul, a full-time and part-time job, an upcoming study abroad trip to Japan, and most importantly an illness in the family in Raleigh—my hometown. Luckily, I was able to travel to Raleigh three times to help my mom's salon clients and take care of other family matters and still go on the study abroad trip to Japan.

I was a fan of Dick after I read his bilingual book twice on the flight to Japan. It was about an immigrant Hispanic girl who grows up in the projects but goes to college and succeeds in the business world. I grew up as a poor immigrant Vietnamese kid, spoke Spanish, and was the first in my entire family to go to grad school. I thought it would be easy to help Dick reach out to kids like me in the community. Perhaps he could help me write *The Networking Diary*? It wouldn't hurt to ask via e-mail.

 April 20
Re: May 18th 1 pm - Atwood Café, Chicago, IL

Dear Dick,

Thank you for your reply. The 18th of May at 1 p.m. will be perfect. We can meet at the café or another place that is most convenient for you.

You will receive a follow-up e-mail prior to the meeting.

I am honored to have the opportunity to meet you soon.

Sincerely,
Nancy

 April 20
Re: May 18th 1 pm - Atwood Cafe, Chicago, IL

Thank you, Nancy. I will look forward to it as well.

YESS! I had worked so hard to get to this point with Dick!!!! Thank you, Tim. Ah! So excited. Before that day, I needed to make sure to have all my book information printed to maximize the meeting. It needed to look professional. It would also need to be in a nice and easy-to-read booklet that he could take with him. Packaging would be just as important as the pitch.

Shoot! I called the restaurant to reserve a table and found out that they close at 1 p.m. on the day of our meeting. Dick was going to kill me for changing times!

May 14
Re: May 18th Please choose time change - Atwood
Café, Chicago, IL

Dick,

I am truly looking forward to meeting with you.

I just called the restaurant to book our reservation and Atwood opens at 11:30 a.m., therefore:

1. We can meet there at 11:00 a.m. in Atwood's lounge

2. We can meet at 11:30 a.m. at Atwood's reception for the cafe

Let me know what is best for you, and I am more than happy to accommodate.

Sincerely,
Nancy

May 14
Re: May 18th Please choose time change - Atwood
Cafe, Chicago, IL

lounge is fine - thanks!

Dick

May 17
Re: May 18th Please choose time change - Atwood Cafe, Chicago, IL

Nancy,

Another member of our staff will be joining us tomorrow to listen in. Her name is Mandy. I hope that is okay.

Thanks,
Dick

 May 17
Re: It would be a pleasure to meet Mandy

Good morning, Dick,

Thank you for your message. It would be a pleasure to meet Mandy.
The more the merrier. I enjoy learning from other outstanding professionals.

Have a wonderful day,
Nancy

Since Tim connected Dick and me in the first place, I sent Tim an update to let him know about the meeting.

May 18
Re: Meeting with Dick today

Dear Tim,

Thank you for the connection to Dick. I am very excited to meet him today at 11 a.m. I spent the entire night perfecting our presentation of *The Networking Diary* to share. You will be proud of the progress.

Nancy

 May 18
Re: Meeting with Dick today

I am excited for you, Nancy.
Please let me know how it goes.

Tim

The night before, I tried to perfect my book proposal by adding graphics and printing everything out in color. I was so excited to meet this Hollywood writer and actor!

The pleasant person Dick was on the phone a few months back does not show up to the meeting. His assistant Mandy arrived at the café first, and we chatted for a few minutes before Dick rushed in. We were seated in the middle of the café, and he didn't even crack a smile.

He looked me in the eye and started the conversation with, "I am at your disposal. What do you want from me?" After his opening statement, I lost my train of thought but tried to hang on to my composure, which was like holding water in my hands. His words, *"I am at your disposal"* meant, *"You have the floor, so take charge and lead this meeting since you scheduled it!"*

I gave him the 30-second pitch I had rehearsed.

"Thank you for meeting today, Dick. I am a big fan of your English/Spanish book and was hoping that you could give pointers on how I can publish a book as successful as yours."

He began to lay into me, and my heart sank. In the meeting, I thought he was going to share the services his publishing company provides to help me with *The Networking Diary*. Wrong. So wrong. My eyes began to look up in the corners of my head as I tried so hard to look for intelligent things to say.

Dick pointed two fingers at me in front of Mandy and yelled, "Hey you! Over here!" and pointed those same fingers at his eyes. My eyes grew bigger, and my fingers began to sweat as I clenched the book proposal I had worked on all night. This was NOT the kind of meeting I had been expecting. Tim is the sweetest man ever, and I would not have imagined that his friend would make me feel like I was being dunked in a tank of water over and over again. I grew up with a militant dad and am used to some old-school disciplinary talk, but I have never had a CEO treat me like a piece of sh*t.

I answered all of his tough questions as best as I knew how to during this dreadful meeting. He hated everything I said and thought that the work I had brought him was terrible. For the questions I was unsure about, I simply responded with, "I am new to this world of publishing and want to learn from the best, like you."

Dick said, "Well, if that is what you want, go to another company, put your book on the shelves, and earn 10% of whatever they sell."

In defense, I said, "But that is not what I want! I want to touch lives and dedicate my time and resources to help people the way your books have."

"It will take five years!" Dick explained.

I squinted my eyebrows and said, "Fine! I will take five years!"

He responded several times with, "Well, what you do you want from me? Huh? What do you want from me?"

In my mind, I thought, *Well, he's the one with the publishing company. Isn't he going to pitch me his services? I guess that he doesn't have to. Who am I? Just some little girl with an idea for a book he doesn't give a damn about.*

The only thing I could think of to respond with was, "I want to be like some of your other authors who have published a book that can reach out to people and help them. If you don't mind me asking, what does five years look like? I think I can do this."

He gave me a time line of what five years to write a book looked like. Then he said, "Send me three sample diary chapters via e-mail, and I will take a look." Dick got up from the table. I thanked him for meeting with me, and abruptly he left. What the hell? I hopped on the train home and felt like I'd been beaten up by the biggest bully in school. When I got home, I busted out in tears and thought, *Should I tell Tim what a mean person his friend is?*

No. A simple thank you would do.

May 18
Re: Cannot thank you enough

Dear Tim,

The meeting with Dick went well. Your recommendation to meet him was spot on, and I cannot thank you enough for this introduction.

He has vision and has pushed me to better understand what is ahead of me with writing this book. I am ready to work as hard as I can to achieve success.

Have a wonderful time in Michigan. When I get back from visiting my mom and dad in June, we will reconnect.

Warmest thoughts,
Nancy

DIARY ENTRY LEARNING LESSONS

Unfortunately, I went home crying and thinking, *I just had my ass handed to me!*

Before you go and meet a new referral, clarify what it is that you want and need and the type of opportunities you are looking for. I was clearly *not* prepared for this meeting with Dick. My assumption was that he was going to meet to pitch his publishing company's services to me. Since I was the one who invited him, I should have come prepared with intelligent questions to lead the meeting. Instead, I wasted his time, and he let me know.

1. Do your research. Use social networking sites and Google to track a person via the media, their professional portfolios, and their postings. I looked up Dick's profile on LinkedIn, read about him in several articles, and asked Tim about Dick. My goal for researching Dick should have been to find out his vision, mission, and short or long-term goals.

2. Use LinkedIn. I looked Dick up on LinkedIn and learned more about him. In addition to his past work experience, I should have looked closer at the groups he belongs to and his interests.

3. Consider the speaker. Although I thought I was knowledgeable about Dick since I looked him up beforehand, I failed to prepare for the meeting with information about what his goals are. Knowing Dick's needs and interests is a very important part of the networking process. In other networking opportunities, you can consider the speaker by offering to pick him or her up from the airport, bringing something, or offering to show him or her around after the meeting.

EXERCISE

The next time you meet with someone, prepare with the following questions:

1. What is this person's vision, mission, and short- or long-term goal?

2. What are the groups this person belongs to, and what are his or her interests?

Ready to network? Now that you know how to prepare for a networking event, get out there and start making connections!

NETWORKING DIARY PRINCIPLE 4

VALUE YOUR CONTACT'S TIME

The key is in not spending time, but in investing it. –Stephen R. Covey

In the fast-paced and high-tech world we live in today, email, text messaging, Twitter, Facebook, and LinkedIn may seem like they can replace just simply meeting with people. Although I am virtually connected with people globally, I still think that face-to-face meetings are valuable. In a face-to-face meeting, you have the opportunity to see body language and get immediate feedback to your questions. Whether you are in person, on Skype, or in a video conference meeting, you have the opportunity to respond with, "I see, but what about . . . ?" or "Can you elaborate more?" or "What do think about . . . ?" type questions. I generally get a lot more information about the person or the opportunity every time I can make eye contact and respond in real-time.

Whether I connect to a person with email or in person, showing that I value their time demonstrates that I am a dependable contact. Today, a combination of face-to-face meetings, phone calls, and the use of the Internet is necessary to maintaining relationships with your contacts. In doing so, it is important to always value your contact's time by respectfully keeping meetings, phone calls, and e-mails brief.

Networking Diary Entry
March 15

Earlier, I shared with you the face-to-face meeting with Dick, the Hollywood writer and actor. The following entries show how he taught me another hard lesson via e-mail about respecting your contact's time.

March 15
Re: Your energy is amazing

Dear Dick,

Your energy in your LinkedIn status is amazing. We need more passionate people like you for positive changes. I met with your friend Tim yesterday and told him that you really like the book about networking.

I am pleased to share that the "networking tool" is progressing. This Thursday, I am headed to Japan with DePaul. When I return in April, I will show you the exciting progress on the writing.

Have a wonderful week, and I look forward to touching base soon.

Sincerely,
Nancy

March 15
Re: Your energy is amazing

Dear Nancy,

Thank you Nancy - I finally mailed you my book about an hour ago! You should get it before your trip.

I look forward to hearing from you when you return.

Travel safely,
Dick

 March 17
Re: Your Book Arrived

Dear Dick,

Your book arrived just in time for Japan. Thank you so much. I am very excited to read it. Someone else already wants to read it, too. In fact, I will try to get everyone on the trip to go buy it when we get back to the States.

Today, I was at DePaul's Barnes and Noble telling the manager about the networking book. She said, "Let's set up a book signing here." The book is not even done and people are already wanting to read it.

When I get back, we'll set up a time to meet. It will be fun.

Enjoy your Guinness,
Nancy

After Dick and I met in person at a café in downtown Chicago, he asked me to send three sample writings from this book.

May 26
Re: The three "Diary" entries you requested

Dear Dick,

Attached you will find the three "Diary" entries that:

- are many levels deeper than the sample you initially saw
- answer your question, "Is this the best lesson?"

I cannot express my gratitude enough for you taking time to review these prototypes for *The Networking Diary*.

Thank you in advance. Looking forward to your feedback.

Sincerely,
Nancy

Dick told me that he would be in New York for a book expo for a while and would send edits when he returned. I waited a few weeks and didn't hear from him. He is a busy man, but he did promise to review the writing pieces I sent him. So I decided to send him an e-mail reminder.

June 11
Re: Your feedback for the three "Diary" entries you requested

Dear Dick,

Hopefully, you enjoyed the book expo in New York a couple of weeks ago.

You mentioned that you would review *The Networking Diary* samples upon your return.

When you have time in the next couple of weeks, I truly look forward to your feedback.

Have a wonderful weekend,
Nancy

 June 11
Re: Your feedback for the three "Diary" entries you requested

Nancy,

Thanks for the reminder! Sorry. Hectic couple weeks. I will get to it shortly!

Dick

Dick and I exchanged e-mails with ideas and sample edits for this book. He is a busy man, and unless I gave him reminders, he would forget to send me what he promised. A business friend told me that when given deadlines, people try to meet them. I figured that in my next e-mail, I could suggest a deadline.

June 17
Re: Please provide feedback by Wednesday 6/21

Dear Dick,

Attached you will find the sample chapter for *The Networking Diary*.
Your feedback has been applied to the shortened version.
I look forward to hearing your feedback by Wednesday (6/21).

Thank you in advance,
Nancy

June 17
Re: Please provide feedback by Wednesday 6/21
(Networking Diary)

Nancy,

I have received your email. I believe that I am offering you the favor of looking over your work. If you'd like to cover my fee of $210 an hour, I'd be happy to guarantee a response by the time provided. If you're expecting this as a favor, I recommend you reword your request.

Dick

Ouch. He was mad! I never thought that something like requesting a completion date would generate such a tone. Dick's message arrived to my Blackberry while I was having a drink at the bar and getting an autograph from my favorite country singer. Despite all the VIP fun I was having, I began to tear up because I hadn't meant to anger my contact. He was right. He was only trying to do me a favor, and I had the nerve to suggest a deadline. This warranted a fast response and apology for disrespecting his time!

 June 17
Re: Completely agree with you

Dear Dick,

You are completely right. My opinion is in alignment with yours. Today, I was in an eight-hour writing seminar and this type of subject line was taught to us. Unfortunately, I immediately applied the lesson and it came off wrong.

Honestly, I have never written a subject line like that in my life, but I combined the lessons drilled today with my deadline to you.

Please accept my apology. Your time is very valuable, and I know better than to disrespect it. I know better to always use professionalism, common sense, and intuition instead of what someone else says.

Sincerely,
Nancy

I wanted to cry. Seriously, Dick was way too important to piss off. He had every right to say what he did. When things are free and from a friend of a CEO, I'm HIS subordinate. MY reputation was on the line with Dick, TIM, and who knows who else. I was in a lot of trouble, and Dick could ruin my tie with Tim. This was NOT good. I hoped that Dick would understand what happened and would be forgiving.

In four days, he responded.

June 21
Re: Completely agree with you

Nancy,

This was much better. See my notes and work to apply them here and to other pieces in the manuscript. You want to concentrate more on showing than telling. Lead us to think you're clever rather than telling us you are, for example. If you lead us there, you become clever in our minds. If you tell us, you come off as arrogant. We do not want to read about or take advice from someone we consider obnoxious or arrogant.

There are other notes in the text as well for you to consider.

Good luck with it!
Dick

Good luck...I guess he was done with helping me.

June 21
Re: Thank you for your notes

Dear Dick,

Your notes have been read several times. The focus will be to avoid using "empty" words like "deflating."

You helped me realize that I need to tell the reader "1+1" instead of "2" so that they can form the answer in their minds.

While writing this piece, I sunk down in my chair and covered my face because humility is important to me.

Thank you for kindly offering the feedback to use for other pieces. I will continue with the steps you described during our face-to-face meeting.

Sincerely,
Nancy

The only times that Dick ever contacted me again was when it was in regards to supporting his charities. Dick is probably the only "bridge" that I lit on fire during business school. Granted, he wasn't the sweetest man in the world, but he did teach me a hard lesson about knowing my limitations in asking for help. Ever since his e-mail from June 17, I have made sure to show my connection how much I value his or her time by giving something back.

A couple of months later, Tim, the CEO mentor who referred Dick to me, asked if I was still working with Dick on this book.

Date: August 1
Re: How is the project?

Good morning Nancy,

Please, at your convenience, tell me more about the book project. Are you still working with Dick?

Thomas

What should I say? *The relationship did not work out.* No, you should never say anything back about a contact you are given. It is not good to bring any negativity into networking. Instead, I sent him a sample of this book with all the edits that Dick provided.

Date: August 3
Re: The Networking Diary

Dear Tim,

Here is a small sample of *The Networking Diary*.

Sincerely,
Nancy

Date: August 3
Re: The Networking Diary

Nancy,

I like your table of contents. Dick's work seems a little bold.

Thomas

Dick's edits were "bold" to say the least. He was not a nice man, like Tim. However, he did teach me the importance of valuing your contact's time and of being prepared. I never told Tim how mean I thought his friend was because preserving dignity is important in business networking. When wronged, mistreated, or otherwise upset in some way, always choose to handle the dispute with finesse. I chose to approach Dick and Tim via calm and private conversations.

DIARY ENTRY LEARNING LESSONS

Since Dick spent his time networking with me, he wanted to get a return on his networking investment, right? I call it his Return on Networking (R.O.N). I failed to create a mutually beneficial relationship with Dick and was not able to offer him value, knowledge, and support over time. While creating your mutually beneficial relationships, you must focus on the businesses and interests of other people while engaging them in enjoyable conversations.

1. Give first by taking the time to gather information about the other person and really understand how you can help them. While building the relationship with Dick, I should have asked more about his business, as well as the challenges he might be facing and how I could help him. Active listening can help me find out if I can introduce Dick to a possible partner or business opportunity; offer a great resource that can benefit him; or provide information, advice, and contacts.

2. Pay it forward. If it were not possible for me to offer Dick anything, this may not have been the best time to start and build a long-term relationship. Since my CEO mentor connected Dick to me, in the short term it is okay to accept help without being able to "repay" Dick right away; however, I should at least let Dick know that I'd really like to repay him for his time. If there is nothing I can "repay" him with at the time, I can at least tell him that I am grateful for his time and that I will pay it "forward" by helping others.

3. Choose your requests gracefully. As a Southerner, I was raised to choose my words carefully. However, to write to tell Dick, "*I look forward to hearing your feedback by Wednesday (6/21)*" is not the way to get something back in a timely manner—especially when he is volunteering his time to do a favor for his friend by helping me! The request should have kept Dick in the driver seat to create opportunities for further conversations. A better ending in the e-mail to Dick is, "*Thank you for taking the time out of your busy schedule to offer your professional*

expertise. I look forward to hearing from you when you have time. In the meantime, please let me know how I can ever help you with anything." Networking is a process, and quick demands rarely lead to a long-term business relationship. The real value in networking happens in follow-ups over time.

EXERCISE

Remember, when someone is doing you a favor, take the time to find out what their needs are.

1. Think if you can introduce your contact to a possible partner or business opportunity; offer a great resource that can benefit him or her; or provide information, advice, and contacts.

2. Allow the person who helps you to control the way they spend their time helping you.

NETWORKING DIARY PRINCIPLE 5

FOLLOW UP OR FORGET IT

I collect human relationships very much the way others collect fine art. –Jerzy Kosinski

The art of networking is based on the premise of giving to others more so than immediately getting something in return. Relationship building after meeting your connection takes care and commitment. You must plant seeds and take ample time to grow the seeds through follow-ups. I enjoy acknowledging the initial contact by setting up a luncheon meeting and learning more about the contact's background and business. To cultivate relationships, I have sent "congratulations" e-mails, shared articles and websites, and given contacts, as promised.

It takes work to organize your contacts and remember what you have promised to whom. Here is a story about how missing a follow-up caused hard feelings and ambiguous room for negative interpretation.

Networking Diary Entry
June 22

Over the winter, Dr. Guy teaches our graduate level Human Resources (HR) classes at DePaul's Kellstadt Graduate School of Business in downtown Chicago. He has done high-level consulting work globally, particularly in the field of employee performance management. My boss charged me with a project to develop a Performance Appraisal for our firm. This was my first time taking on this kind of project. It made sense to ask for help from a professor with knowledge about this topic. Hopefully, Dr. Guy would offer his expertise.

June 22
Re: Performance Appraisal

Dr. Guy:

I took your Global HR class in December. To-day, I read your White Paper about performance evaluation while doing research for my firm. Would you have about 15 mins. to answer some questions I have about standardized performance management?

Attached is a draft of an outline that I think I will be building on. Basically, my firm has never had a standardized performance evaluation process, and I am trying to review the system that will be implemented, review best practices, and offer recommendations.

If you are available, I can either meet on campus any day after 5pm or call you any time. I look forward to hearing from you.

Thank you,
Nancy

June 22
Re: Performance Appraisal

Nancy,

You can call me on my mobile anytime. Noted that your firm is apparently working with a similar firm, so it may be wise to talk to them. Conflicting views from consultants can cause confusion. But am happy to answer any questions you have.

Dr. Guy

July 3
Re: Stuff for you

Nancy,

To add to your confusion, attached are my Book Intro and the two chapters dealing with performance management. You have seen some of the material from class, but this is the most up-to-date.
Let me know how you progress.

Dr. Guy

July 3
Re: Stuff for You

Dr. Guy:

Thank you so much! I like all this confusion; it means that I am learning. This is so neat that my firm is trying to make these changes. When I see you again, I would like a few more of your business cards to give to our executives.

Talk to you soon,
Nancy

 July 4
Re: Favorite Philosophy

Nancy,

Oliver Wendel Holmes once said, "I would give nothing for simplicity this side of complexity; I would give everything for simplicity the other side of complexity."

Anyone who thinks performance management is simple is being simplistic.

Dr. Guy

July 4
Re: Favorite Philosophy

Dr. Guy:
Something to think about this holiday week-end. I think that I am going to post this quote on my desk. Thank you for sharing and helping me set realistic expectations for the boss.

Happy 4th,
Nancy

July 15
Re: Performance Evaluation Process

Dear Dr. Guy:

Despite all of the changes that have taken place here at my firm. The boss is still eager to roll out a performance evaluation system. Attached is what I recreated based on the materials you gave me.

Do you mind providing feedback and rec-ommendations for the next steps? I have also provided the leaders here with your contact information.

Thank you,
Nancy

July 15
Re: Performance Evaluation Process

Nancy,

Think you have done a great job. Looks good—certainly better than what you had before.

If the folks down there want a small amount of guidance, I am available. By the way, due to federal contracts my least and best rate is $200 per hour, and I would be willing to extend that to the firm even though current contracts are at $250-300 per hour. I do have a vested interest in the firm doing well.

Let me know if you need more information. How about a few more books? Seriously, what you have is the best available and totally adequate.

Dr. Guy

 July 16
Re: Performance Evaluation Process

Dr. Guy,

I will read any book that you tell me is good. On Friday, we will be meeting with the boss to discuss our projects. I will update you with what the boss says.

Have a wonderful day!

Thank you,
Nancy

Dr. Guy and I spoke via phone about the plans to roll out the performance appraisals. He was as excited to work with my bosses as I was to learn how to customize a Performance Appraisal for our employees. During the summer, I provided several edits to the Performance Appraisal forms with my boss and Dr. Guy.

When classes started again in September, I learned about a scholarship for students interested in majoring in Human Resources (HR). Since Dr. Guy understood how much I dedicated to a career in HR, I figured he'd write me a solid recommendation.

September 8
Re: Request for letter for reference for HR Graduate Scholarship

Dear Dr. Guy,

I am writing to ask whether it would be possible for you to provide me with a reference for an HR scholarship.

If you are able to verify my qualifications and provide insight into my educational goals, work ethic, values, personality, and need for the scholarship, I would sincerely appreciate it.

I am in the process of applying for the graduate scholarship, and a positive reference from you would enhance my prospects of achieving my career goals.

Please let me know if there is any information I can provide regarding my experience to assist you in giving me a reference. Attached is my resume and essay if you would like to refer to them. Thank you for your consideration.

Reference letters may be 1-2 pages in length and should be addressed to the Review Committee.

Letters should be in .pdf or Word format and should include your signature. Deadline: October 15.

Sincerely,
Nancy

 September 8
Re: Request for letter for reference for HR Gradu-
ate Scholarship

Nancy,

Am happy to do so. Will work on that over the next several days. By the way, in your resume under your firm, you mention EAPs. These are "employee assistance programs," not "employee assistant programs," as you currently state. Think you should make that change so someone carefully examining your resume does not pick it up.
Will get back to you. Keep motoring.

Dr. Guy

 October 20

Nancy,

You can forward this electronically to the HR scholarship committee. Have lost the address I am supposed to use. Headed out to Middle East shortly.
Congratulations on the success with your firm's Performance Appraisal form. Tell your boss

we will be useful in guiding your firm with the roll out of the Performance Appraisals.

Dr. Guy

From June to October (four months), Dr. Guy graciously helped our firm with the Performance Appraisal form and me with the HR Graduate Scholarship. At that point in my career, I was able to quickly get things done by going out, getting the resources I needed, and executing the projects well. My bosses appreciated it, and I was able to build my network through connecting people to each other. In the meantime, my schedule filled with travel, more projects, classes, and more networking, and Dr. Guy sent me a valid complaint after not hearing from me for five months.

 March 10
Re: Complaint

Nancy,

Wanted to complain about the heavy workload we have been experiencing with your firm on the Performance Appraisals . . . need more pay if we are going to work this hard. Seriously, I presume that concept was dissolved in the political acid pot. The media detailed the travesties going on with the slush funds of your firm, which would seem to warrant cleanup if the past court indictments are to be addressed. But what do I know?

Hope all is well with you. Never heard any more from HR Graduate Scholarship, so I presume they got everything from me on your scholarship application . . . whatever happened with it?

Stay in touch. Don't get down there unless I am teaching or there is a need. Glad to have coffee some time though.

Bill Guy

Damn it! It is RARE that I make a vital mistake not to follow up! I pride myself on keeping in touch with people, even since elementary school. How dare I forget about Dr. Guy? I mean, he only donated thousands of dollars worth of help to get me through the biggest project I had for the firm. He only busted his ass to write me a letter of recommendation for an HR Graduate Scholarship. Quite frankly, when I lost interest in a career in HR, his e-mails were accidentally "grouped in" with the ones I deleted.

Not remembering to follow up with your contacts is a common mistake in the world of networking. It is good that Bill had a dry sense of humor, but boy was I in a lot of trouble with him. DAMN IT. Mistakes like these are unacceptable at the beginning stages of networking, since networking is about building long-term relationships.

March 10
Re: New Boss = Dissolved projects

Dear Dr. Guy,

Your complaints are valid. Since the appointment of the new boss in December, all of the previous projects dissolved. I would love to tell you more in person.

I apologize for not touching base, but I promise to keep you posted. I am normally really good about keeping in touch, but my mom was hospitalized in Raleigh, NC with a liver abscess. I have since resigned from the firm and have been flying between Chicago and Raleigh to help keep her salon business afloat.

My dad and I are on our way to meet with our CPA about taxes, NC, so I will write more this evening.

Thank you,
Nancy

 March 10
Re: Your Very Delayed and Deserved Follow up

Dear Guy,

You certainly deserve a follow-up. In fact, I am embarrassed that I have not done so. Usually, I am on top of this. Here are some updates:

Graduate HR Scholarship

Unfortunately, the selection committee did not select me as one of the scholarship recipients. It is assumed that the candidate pool was large and competitive. Your letter was fantastic, but without a 4.0 GPA, it probably knocked me out of the pool. Your letter only strengthened the application; however, I was humbled to receive DePaul's Dr. John N. Nicholson Scholarship. He was an immigrant who became very successful here in the States. I truly hope that my immigrant background will continue to push me to work hard.

Firm Change

I resigned from the firm on good terms. My mom's business in Raleigh has been my priority right now. Additionally, I have been working with other entrepreneurs, attending angel investor meetings, and working in an entrepreneurship incubator. It has lit a fire in my soul to work with other entrepreneurs. You understand because you are also a very successful entrepreneur.

Japan & Book I am writing

Next week, I am headed to Japan with DePaul. When I get back, I am going to complete *The Networking Diary* that I have been compiling. It is intended to share real life stories and results of networking, offer tools/principles for modern day networking, and show the intimate side of it. For example, my delay of following up with you is a networking "no-no." I have been listening carefully to my "audience," and they seem excited to have a tool like this.

Your Schedule

Are you in the country? It would be wonderful to meet for a quick bite or coffee soon. You have been all over the world, and I would love to hear about what is on your plate and what you have planned next. Again, I would like to apologize for being your bad protégé. When we get together, I will also tell you more about the experience at my firm.

Please let me know what your schedule is next week or during the first week of April (after Japan).

Sincerely,
Nancy

March 10
Re: Your Very Delayed and Deserved Follow up

Nancy,

Guess you are not suffering from boredom. Don't know if I have to go to NM next week, but if not I will contact you and coffee could be an idea.
Sorry to hear about the family medical challenges, and I wish you the best outcome.

Dr. Guy

 March 10
Re: Your Very Delayed and Deserved Follow up

Dear Dr. Guy,

Thank you for your e-mail. Coffee with you would be fantastic.
I can only imagine how many airline miles you acquire a year.
Have a great week, and I hope that next week will work.

Sincerely,
Nancy

Since Dr. Guy helped me on a major project, he should have received updates about changes that took place. For example, there were changes in leadership. My first boss resigned and another person filled his position. That boss was demoted, and the third boss did not have the time to focus on the project.

I should also have graciously thanked Dr. Guy for writing the letter of recommendation after I found out that I was not selected as a recipient. His e-mails made me aware of how poorly I had networked with him. I failed to find out more about his needs so that I could try to fill them. Without this mutually beneficial relationship, it was hard for me to remember to remain in contact. I needed to meet with him as soon as possible to rekindle this professional relationship. This time around, I would need to keep e-mails short, ask more questions about him, and find out how I might help him with his current goals.

March 16
Re: Are you in NM?

Good morning, Dr. Guy,

Are you taking over the skies again this week?
If so, have a wonderful trip and we'll chat soon.

Yours truly,
Nancy

No response was sent by Dr. Guy for weeks. I'd really burned this bridge and was trying to replay how I'd lost contact with him. This was awful. He is one of the top HR professionals in Chicago, and I had been completely unprofessional because I forgot to touch base with him about our unfinished projects, current happenings, or to simply ask if I could do anything for him. I decided I would try again in a few weeks.

April 2
Re: Your Availability

Dear Dr. Guy,

Are you in town during the upcoming weeks? I just returned from Japan with the DePaul seminar and would love to see you. Any Monday-Thursday would be great if you are available.

Have a great day,
Nancy

April 2
Re: Your Availability

Nancy,

Am out the next two weeks but should be in town the 19th. Let me know if that works.

Dr. Guy

April 2
Re: Your Availability

Dr. Guy,

Thank you for your response.
Would you be available for lunch or coffee on April 19th? Your choice: 12:30 lunch or 4:00 coffee.

Nancy

 April 2
Re: Your Availability

Nancy,

Let's do a 12:30 lunch on the 19th. Meet you in the Management Dept.

Dr. Guy

 April 2
Re: Your Availability

Dr. Guy,

Perfect. See you then. Safe travels.

Nancy

It does not hurt to follow up, follow up, follow up! A couple of days before our meeting, I sent him a follow-up to confirm the date, time, location, and to let him know that I looked forward to seeing him soon.

We ate at Exchequer, and on the way in he asked me, "Do you own the place?" since everyone greeted me by name. Exchequer was my favorite bar and pizza place near DePaul's downtown campus. The DePaul MBA Association frequently held networking events there.

I was tired, but the lunch meeting with Dr. Guy went well. During our lunch, I found out many new updates about him. He had just published an HR book about Employee Performance. I found out about his current projects, his travels, and his future goals. We talked about everything from business to baseball. He was in his 70s but had tons of energy. Dr. Guy is a world-class HR professional. He's also the one who yelled at me for not keeping in touch with him. Bad Nancy!

We then talked about *The Networking Diary.* He liked the ideas behind the book. I also shared my business ideas for my Sweet T brand. He liked the Southern brand idea and said to just continue to do what I love. He also suggested that a PhD for me would be good in the next ten years. Something to think about…

While trying to figure out what I could do for him, I learned that he wanted more business students to mentor. After brainstorming, I told him I would try to connect him to DePaul's Coleman Entrepreneurship board. Dr. Guy might be a successful worldwide CEO, but he was stuck in the HR circle. I suggested how he could organize seminars for entrepreneurs and other business students.

On a more personal level, our conversation about men was hilarious. I was not dating at the time, and he said, "If I were younger, I'd chase after you." Yikes!

At the end of lunch, we agreed to use LinkedIn to connect with each other. I also promised to promote his book through my LinkedIn status update.

April 21
Re: Nancy Nguyen, MBA has indicated you are a
Colleague at DePaul University Kellstadt School of
*Business: via**LinkedIn***

Dr. Guy,

As mentioned, your book is featured on my profile. I'd like to add you to my professional network on LinkedIn. Please take a moment and accept my invitation.

Thank you,
Nancy

A couple of months later, Dr. Guy sent an e-mail to the people in his professional circle and included me.

June 21
Re: New Material

You are invited to visit my website for the most up-to-date weather and news. Failing that, I hope you might find a book you need. But most of all, I encourage dialogue about all that interests us.
Hope to be in touch soon.
Dr. Guy

Throughout the year, I sent Dr. Guy several follow-up e-mails:

 June 21
Re: New Material

Dear Dr. Guy

Thank you for sharing your new site with us. It looks great.
Will you be adding any links to Facebook or Twitter?
I hope to see you sometime this summer.

Sincerely,
Nancy

 January 3
Re: A happy, healthy, and prosperous year to you.

Dr. Guy,

I hope that your New Year's was wonderful.

Warmest,
Nancy

October 12
Re: Hope you are well!

Dear Dr. Guy,

You crossed my mind today.
I hope that you are well.

Sincerely,
Nancy

 October 12
Re: Hope you are well!

Nancy,

Am well indeed. Just got verification that my second book will be published next year. Am working on two more . . . this I believe is the best way to give back to the profession, and I feel honored that I have the opportunity to do so.

Hope you are well and that your energy is still propelling you to be all you can be.

Dr. Guy

October 12
Re: Hope you are well!

Hello Dr. Guy,

Congratulations on your books! Your material has definitely helped me lead diverse groups.

I am completing my book, *The Networking Diary*, this year to help young MBAs network. My Raleigh salon is growing, but I long for Chicago every day. I hope to make it back soon.

Be well, and please keep in touch.

Sincerely,
Nancy

In fact, now that I am talking about Dr. Guy, let's go ahead and send him a follow-up...

December 26
Re: Hope you are well!

Dear Dr. Guy

Hello from Raleigh! Hope that you had a fantastic holiday week and are ready for next year.

Warmest,
Nancy

Wow! Within two minutes, I received a reply.

December 26
Re: Hope you are well!

Nancy,

And a great holiday season to you.

Dr. Guy

DIARY ENTRY LEARNING LESSONS

It is easy to forget to follow-up with people, but just remember that a sincere and meaningful follow up is an investment in your relationship. As a beginner networker, I wanted to meet, connect, and work with many people. Now, I take the time to network with a purpose and build relationships. Dr. Guy understands that I no longer want to follow his career path, but he can count on me to bounce ideas off of, connect him to students, or reach out to my former HR organizations. Even without all the professional bells and whistles, it is nice to touch base with a friend. Networking and friendship-building are similar.

1. You must follow up, not try to. It's one of the quickest ways to set you apart in a positive way. So few people do what they promise at a networking event. Initiate an e-mail, phone call, meeting, or send a relevant article or the referral you promised.

2. Set follow-up reminders in your calendar. Although there is a lot of technology to use, I still like to use my paper planner to write notes. I have seen other people use smartphones or electronic calendars. Super networkers may use sources like Salesforce. com. One time, a professor sent me a Happy Birthday note through LinkedIn. Don't make the mistake I made with Dr. Guy and follow up only when something is needed. That is bad networking.

3. Have a clear goal for follow-ups. A simple message stating why I contacted Dr. Guy helped him understand my goal of connecting. For example, one of my e-mails could have included, "Dr. Guy, Thank you for your recent help. We have had a change in leadership in my department and our project has been put on hold. I will let you know when the new leaders decide to focus on the project." Make sure the person with whom you are networking has a clear understanding of your goals and reasons for wanting to build a relationship. ALSO make sure that you find out how you can help the person with his or her goals. That allows you to offer the person articles, websites, or contacts you may run across in between follow-ups.

EXERCISE

The next time you follow up with someone, think:

1. What is this person's current goal or problem to solve? Is there an article, website, or contact I can offer this person?

2. When does this person expect me to meaningfully follow up again?

Take the time to think about people you need to follow up with and let them know that you are available to help.

NETWORKING DIARY PRINCIPLE 6

ALWAYS BE PROFESSIONAL

Holding on to anger is like grasping a hot coal with the intent of throwing it at someone else; you are the one who gets burned. –Buddha

Good networkers can maintain professional communications when faced with the most belligerent trolls in business without letting themselves be goaded into unprofessional behavior. Sometimes my Type-A personality gets in the way, and I become very angry with some of the idiots I run into. However, while networking, you are often the face of your business or organization. Everything you say and do reflects on the organization you represent.

Currently, I serve as our business school's class Executive Vice President and Ambassador. I also serve as the liaison for students at our school and for an outside professional Human Resources (HR) organization. An unprofessional interaction can make me and the organizations I represent look unprofessional in front of executives, clients, and potentially the media; however, staying professional at all times is harder than it sounds. This story I am going to share is about a mentor who bombarded me with negative comments.

Networking Diary Entry
January 5

The current goal of the HR organization I belong to is to "Penetrate Social Media." A recent electronic newsletter from the organization announced that the next workshop would:

> "... *help you get a better understanding of social media and prepare for the inevitable changes it will bring about with the Social Media in Organizations.*
>
> *With so many advocates shouting from their cyber rooftops about social media's virtues, it's easy to forget that the vast majority of folks are still trying to figure out what the hype is all about—and what it means for them and their organizations.*
>
> *To help you get a better understanding of social media and prepare for the inevitable changes it will bring about, our HR organization has joined forces with a Social Media Organization to offer a half-day workshop on February 10 in the morning. This workshop will be a bootcamp of sorts, providing attendees the opportunity to learn by doing—bring your laptop and experiment with different ideas as you hear about them!*"

Great! A couple of years ago, I set up Facebook fan pages for organizations like *American Airlines Admirals Club,* and its pages have attracted nearly 1,000 fans. A marketing manager from American Airlines contacted me to add current photos of the clubs on the fan page I created.

Since the professional HR organization I belonged to noted that they were interested in growing their membership through social media, I customized a fan page for it.

We attracted over 100 fans who then began to exchange professional advice through this Facebook page. Later, someone from the HR Organization e-mailed me about the Facebook fan page.

January 5
Re: Facebook Fan Page

Hi Nancy,

How are you? The Communications Committee has developed a Facebook page for our Members. We would like for you to remove the page that you have set up under the organization's name.

Thank you for your continued efforts to help promote us! Please let me know if you have any additional questions.

Thanks,
Martha

In the world of Facebook, anyone is allowed to create fan pages for an organization, person, or brand. In fact, it is good for the organization to have people voluntarily create multiple positive fan pages because the fans can provide free viral marketing. Many brands, causes, and people have dozens of positive and negative fan pages created by strangers worldwide.

Instead of e-mailing Martha to tell her what a lousy job their Communications Committee was doing in promoting the group, I just ignored her silly request. What if I had been a stranger? There would have been no way that she could have contacted me directly requesting the removal of a public Facebook fan page.

At the end of the month, my mentor within the same HR organization sent me an aggressive e-mail. Her e-mail reflected the attitudes of the people in this HR group about this Facebook fan page.

 January 25
Re: Facebook Fan Page

Hi Nancy,

The headquarters has brought to my attention that you have a Facebook page for our organization. I'm not sure where you got permission to set up a Facebook page on behalf of our group. I have indicated to them that you do not actively participate on the College Relations Committee nor did I authorize you to establish a Facebook page. This was never discussed with me or anyone from the College Relations Committee. I am requesting that you take down the Facebook page.

Thank You!
Jamie

Wow. This is a lady who had always been so kind to me when I saw her on campus. She had also been my reliable mentor in the field of HR. Ms. Jamie does not seem like a pleasant person in this e-mail. Life is too short to be so demandingly negative. I would think HR people—especially my mentor—would be more civil.

Prior to responding with a defensive e-mail, I e-mailed my closest professional HR friends and attached Jamie's e-mail and my initial response to solicit their advice on how to proceed. This is the draft of my letter to Jamie:

Good morning Jamie,

I hope that you have had a wonderful start to your new year. Thank you for your recent e-mail. Your headquarters had failed to understand that you can create positive or negative Fan Pages for anything. For example, I created a fan page for the *American Airlines Admiral Club*. One of their corporate leaders kindly contacted me to collaborate. Now, it is one of the highest ranking fan pages. The American Airlines corporate member has even scheduled to fly up to Chicago to meet with me.

Facebook

You can create a fan page for anything that you believe is a good cause. You also have the same right to create negative messages by venting. In the future, your headquarters needs to realize that more users will create groups sending positive or negative messages through social media. It will be impossible to try and chase users. Fortunately, the UNOFFICIAL SHRP page that took a lot of time to make was intended to:

- Fully support the association
- Increase awareness
- help the organization be as competitive as other associations

Top leaders understand

Any publicity is good publicity. You do not need permission to create any page on Facebook. It is a free site primarily used by a young generation. Organizations that do have exposure of groups created by many students will struggle. Many of my successful business mentors support the creation of Twitter, MySpace, and Facebook accounts. They are unaware of how social media works, but they know that social media is vital to the survival of any organization.

It's actually an UNOFFICIAL Page

This page is also called the UNOFFICIAL fan page. It even directs members to the official page. It has probably drawn a broader and even more influential audience that our HR organization doesn't reach. It is inevitable that more groups and pages will be created by dedicated or angry members in the future.

Clarification

You said that you "have indicated to them that [I] do not actively participate on the College Relations Committee." I want to clarify that the organization has not sent me any e-mails in a very long time. However, like your colleague Jerry, I am one of the most active advocates for the organization within the Kellstadt Graduate School of business.

Dozens of students each month come to me with questions about HR and the benefits of the organization. Although I am not invited to any of your meetings, I have continuously put forth effort to encourage undergraduate and graduate DePaul students to join. With the positions (ambassador, former MBA board member, etc.) that I am in, I am one of the key MBA contacts at DePaul when people have questions about HR. It is unfortunate that in spite of our conversations at several meetings, you do not think that I have continued to be an active member.

Next Social Media Boot Camp

By looking at the organization's current website, the next workshop on February 10 is to "help you get a better understanding of social media and prepare for the inevitable changes it will bring about." In fact, the website says, "With so many advocates shouting from their cyber rooftops about social media's virtues, it's easy to forget that the vast majority of folks are still trying to figure out what the hype is all about—and what it means for them and their organizations."

Positive Page & Proposal

Since our organization is already in the game with exposure on Facebook, I would like to propose a professional compromise:

- The current leaders should become admins on the UNOFFICIAL page
- Use the UNOFFICAL page as an example of positive social media
- Visit the page and see that it has all accurate information
- Understand that it actually directs members to the official page
- Understand that you can create **any** Facebook message you want to support or defame without permission

Recommendation

The organization does not want to anger the current members be simply deleting the group. The group members would find it more beneficial to see a current leader become an active admin. Since this page sheds positive light for the organization, the best thing to do for its members is to have another trusted person act as the UNOFFICIAL page's administrator. To go about that, someone just has to join the group, then ask to be an admin.

If you have any further questions, I would be more than happy to meet or discuss via phone. As you already know, I prefer to maintain positive relations with professional colleagues. Please feel free to call me at my office.

Best regards,
Nancy

I then solicited confidential responses from three of my top mentors. Two of them are heavily involved in the HR community.

January 25
Re: Your Opinion about a Facebook Fan Page

Hi,

I hope that you have had a wonderful January. If you have a chance, may I get your opinion about this LinkedIn message that I received below in the HR community? Your opinion would be greatly appreciated.

Thank you,
Nancy

Response 1 understands my view...

January 25
Re: Your Opinion about a Facebook Fan Page

Hi Nancy - January is good and not too cold... Hope you're doing well.

So...my first reaction is OMG! Really, you are really helping to support their association. The second is that any publicity is good publicity. The third would be this is a perfect example of why these organizations struggle. Why not try to at least meet in the middle.

My hunch is she will become very territorial. So my recommendation is to see if there is a professional compromise. You probably draw a broader and even more influential audience that this organization doesn't reach. If she pushes too hard just gracefully step back. Typically I would say fight and say you have just as much of a right and actually it is helping them more than hurting them. But, my experience in similar groups tells me they just don't get it and your time is better spent partnering and supporting someone that does.

Hope this helps,
Orlando

January 26
Re: Thank you

Orlando,

Thank you for taking the time to respond. Before I drop kick her, see my response. Let me know what you think of my response.

Thank you,
Nancy

January 26
Re: Thank you

Nancy,

I think you are right on and expressed your-self in a very positive way. Hope she gets it.

Orlando

Response 2 discourages me from sending the e-mail to save my reputation...

January 25
Re: Your Opinion about a Facebook Fan Page

Dear Nancy,

Wow Nancy, wow. Do you want my honest opinion of your email? Let's revisit it in person in the near future. In short, most of this should have been discussed on the phone or in person to ensure the appropriate tone is communicated. Additionally, you insulted her intelligence by giving her FB lessons, and I anticipate she will either fire back with aggression, or not respond at all. Beyond that, I think you were appropriate.

Jerry

January 26
Re: Ridiculous

Jerry,

I have not sent it. So if there are any changes, please let me know. She needs all the FB lessons she can get.

Nancy

January 26
Re: Ridiculous

Nance,

I put a lot of thought into this email so please read it slowly, maybe more than once. I care about your reputation and future, so please take heed to my words.

Educating Jamie is not your responsibility to do. I urge you to change the subject line of your email to "A few thoughts." I'd suggest a meeting with the president, or just show up at the "social media" meeting and share your thoughts there. Add value there and you will be recognized. An email isn't the appropriate communication medium to respond and voice frustrations. For one, it can be documented and used against you...to remove you from the organization, or otherwise. Also, my name is out of context in your email to her; please remove it. The last thing I want is her reaching out to me and end up stuck in the middle.

I know that you're angry, but don't make the mistake of acting out of frustration/impulse, please. I don't think that you have an ego problem by any means, but check it at the door. You may be finished with this organization right now because of this, but, they are a powerful resource in the HR community and you don't want to leave a bad taste in their mouth due to a misjudgment. If you lash back, they are going to think that you cannot constructively face confrontation. It may take years to develop trust and credibility but it can be lost with one misjudgment or act. Remember, Jamie is one person, and she is influential in the organization due to her longevity and ability to play political cards. Pose as a friend, work as a spy, and as they say in Godfather pt. 2., "Keep your friends close, and your enemies even closer."

I'm hopping off the computer for a few hours to study. Be cool :)

Jerry

After this response I thought:

1. *Do I want to cover all this information in an email versus phone?*

No. But I don't know what to cut.

2. *Do I want to direct any personal statements back to her?*

Yes, but I shouldn't. I don't know what to cut.

3. *Do I want to include Jerry's name? Is there another person I can include so that I do not point to him?*

No. I cut that out.

4. *Do I want to send my response?*

No.

 January 26
Re: Ridiculous

Jerry,

There was not a subject line create yet. J The original one, "Ridiculous" is just for your e-mail. However, I really like, "A few thoughts."

Instead of educating Jamie, I put, "As you already know…"

It is impossible for me to go to any daytime meetings. So I cannot meet with anyone.

I agree that an email isn't the appropriate communication medium to respond and voice frustrations. Don't worry, your name is completely out of the e-mail. I am still packaging it. Once I get it right, I will send it back to you.

My goal is to make them recognize that deleting the fan page is a bad idea, they cannot chase new creators, and that I am not an enemy.

Anyway, I am going to cut a lot and go from there. It won't be sent until it is nicely packaged.

Thank you,
Nancy

Response 3 encourages me to just pick up the phone and call Jamie…

 January 26

Dear Nancy,

You've done a fine job of formatting your e-mail by writing an excellent Motivation Sentence. Good for you.

You have also stated your case well in your e-mail to Ms. Jamie. Let's think about your message strategy to get what you want.

Your message has two main thoughts; two main elements:

1. Your cogent ideas.

2. Your fight with Ms. Jamie.

Suggestion: Don't try to accomplish both message goals at the same time in the same message. Stage your communication strategy:

Stage one: Win Ms. Benitez's trust and respect. Call her and speak v to v: Because you've got to show your attitude, not your ideas. Your ideas must be held until her attitude toward you is right. Apologize until she's soothed. This may take time. Who's right or wrong does not matter here. You want her to conform to your will and your ideas. She'll not do that in her current state of mind.

Show your good will toward her and her association: Respect, admiration, seek avenues to communicate similarity between you and her (Liking = perceived similarity).

Resist the urge to use your considerable force of personality and intelligence: You'll crush her and scare her off.

Stage Two: Then, build a relationship of doing: your ideas.

As you know from reading Dale Carnegie, the fact that you're right means nothing at this point. The only thing that matters is what Ms. Jamie is feeling toward you.

Give me a call if you'd like to take this further.

Dr. Joel Whalen

January 27

Dear Professor Whalen,

Thank you for providing very helpful advice for the response.

Your advice helped me think about how to communicate with Jamie. I am very happy with the action plan you took the time to offer.

I went ahead and left her a voicemail and hope to speak to her today. When she responds, I will let you know the positive outcome.

Best regards,
Nancy

 January 27

Dear Nancy,

Your e-mail formatting is excellent. You can be proud.

Thank you for taking time to send a briefing on your persuasive communication with Ms. Jamie. It will also be a wonderful chance for you to practice managing your attitude in stressful communication, and, to practice some of the ideas from Dale Carnegie.

Call me anytime, I can back you up.

Dr. Joel Whalen

Thank goodness I had not sent that draft to Jamie. And thank goodness I had close mentors who had my back. It is so important to stay cool, calm, and collected. I can only imagine what the results would have been had I blasted her with my initial response. Instead, I left her a friendly voicemail: *"Hi Jamie, it's Nancy. Thank you so much for your e-mail. When you get a chance, I'd love to chat a bit about your recent e-mail. Have a great day!"* In the meantime, I discovered that the leader of the HR organization ALSO went to DePaul for Business School thirty years ago. Yay! Hopefully, common thread would be my "in" with him. I decided to e-mail him since Jamie hadn't yet responded to my voicemail.

January 27
Re: Hello from DePaul & Your HR Organization

Dear Mr. BJ,

Your level of expertise in business and HR is very impressive. Since you are a profound leader of your HR organization and the Chicago business community, I would like to have the opportunity to ask about strategic partnerships.

I was the Executive Vice President last year for the DePaul MBA Association and currently serve as an ambassador for the DePaul Kellstadt Graduate School of Business. I would like to know how I can help you with a strategic partnership.

There has been a concern that was recently brought up to me about your HR organization, and I would like to discuss it with you in confidence. When you have a moment, I would be honored to have a moment to meet with you for lunch or coffee about:
* Strategic partnerships

* A recent concern about your HR organization

* Your MBA experience

Thank you for taking the time to accept my e-mail.

Sincerely,
Nancy

Jamie still hadn't returned my phone call or e-mail, but the director contacted me. He is a law partner, a De-Paul MBA grad, and the director of the HR organization. Although he did not know me, he invited me to join a conference call in regards to the Facebook page I created for the group.

 January 27
Re: Hello from DePaul & Your HR Organization

Hello,

I could be available tomorrow to talk over the telephone around 2:00 p.m. I am not back downtown until next week, if talking in person is preferable.

BJ

January 27
Re: Hello from DePaul & Your HR Organization

Mr. BJ,

Thank you for your quick reply. Tomorrow at 2:00 p.m. would be great. If anything changes, please let me know. I am more than happy to work around your busy schedule. I look forward to speaking with you.

Thank you,
Nancy

January 28
Re: Hello from DePaul & Your HR Organization

Hello Nancy,

Our HR Organization's strategic partnerships are group efforts, and so we will have additional participants in the conversation. I am providing a teleconference line to facilitate the discussion. Please call at 2:00 P.M today.

BJ

The call started promptly at 2 p.m. To my surprise, there were three other directors on the call. It was very stressful to present my point of view to all the angry people.

I did my best to navigate through all the negativity. I happily suggested that they take over the Facebook fan page that I had created. Ironically, they were trying to run a Social Media Boot Camp the next day. I suggested that they should use the unofficial Facebook fan page as a supplement to the boot camp. The people on the call continued to huff and puff and be angry with me even at the end of the call. I just kept smiling and suggesting positive things to help them use social media, like a Facebook fan page, to grow the organization. They didn't care. They just wanted to take back what I'd created and shut it down by deleting it.

The call really turned me off, and I would never join this organization again. The American Airlines Admirals Club Facebook fan page I initially created has thousands of members because they kindly collaborated and took the initiative to grow the page.

After the call, one of the directors on the call wanted to meet with me for lunch to learn how to use the unofficial Facebook fan page.

 January 28
Re: Phone conference

Nancy,

Thank you for sharing your ideas with us today. I did request to join the unofficial Facebook fan page so you can give me administration access once you see it.

I want to confirm our plan to get together February 2nd, at 12:30. I will come to your office so we can continue our discussion and see how we can put your ideas into action.

Thanks again for being willing to transition the unofficial Facebook page to us for future operation.

Gi Gi, PHR

 January 28
Re: 11th floor at my building

Dear Gi Gi,

Thank you for amazing energy today. Your positivity was very appreciated. Although I was unaware about who was going to be on the call, I felt that the call was successful. Your name does not come up on the Facebook Page, but I will try and revisit it again over the weekend and make you the director.
When you come to my office on Tuesday, we will walk to lunch and chat for about 45 minutes. Have a good weekend, and I will see you soon.

Warmest,
Nancy

 February 8
Subject: Reschedule Tuesday lunch

I am sorry to say that I need to reschedule our lunch for Tuesday. Are you planning to go to the networking on the 11th? If so maybe we can meet before then.

Otherwise let me know what would work for you.

Thanks
Gi Gi, PHR

February 8
Re: Reschedule Tuesday lunch

Dear Gi Gi,

Thank you for your e-mail. No problem at all. Would you like to reschedule for one day next Tuesday-Friday during lunch?

Sincerely,
Nancy

February 10
Re: Friday meeting about your recommendations for Your HR Organization

Nancy,

I may be downtown Friday for a meeting that is yet to be set up. Would you be available at any point then?

Let me know,
Gi Gi, PHR

February 11
Re: Friday meeting about your recommendations

Nancy,

I will let you know the next time I am in the loop and see if we can find a time that works for both of us.

In the meantime, if there is anything I can do for you, don't hesitate to ask.

Gi Gi, PHR

February 13
RE: Friday meeting about your recommendations

Gi Gi,

Please do. It would be a pleasure to meet with you for lunch when it is convenient for you. Have a wonderful Valentine's weekend.

Sincerely,
Nancy

Gi Gi nor anyone in the HR organization ever wanted to meet with me to hear how to use the unofficial Facebook fan page to continue to grow membership. All they wanted was to control the organization by deleting anything anyone created through social media that was related to the organization. Months later, I received an e-mail to renew my membership, and I just deleted it. I refuse to be part of an organization that does not foster creativity and innovation. The conference call with three surprise guests who threw me under the bus did not make the organization attractive to me either.

I never heard from Jamie. She completely betrayed me by telling the organization negative things about me, and she never returned my call. I sent her an e-mail after the conference call, and she responded one month later.

January 28
Re: Follow up on voicemail

Dear Jamie,

Hello! How are you? I hope that your week has been good and that you have been able to keep warm. I am just following up on the voicemail that I left for you this week.

You will be pleased to know that your organization's leaders will be the official admin of the Facebook page. It will be a very positive experience. If you have a chance and would like to clarify anything, you can reach me via phone/e-mail.

Warmest regards,
Nancy

February 3
Re: Follow up on voicemail

Hi Nancy,

I'm glad things worked out. Thank You!

Jamie

Diary Entry Learning Lessons

Don't bad-mouth people. You never know how that can come back to haunt you. A disparaging remark about Jamie can make people think that I lack business savviness and sense. Am I angry at her for throwing me under the bus in front of a board of directors? Sure. It is inevitable that some people can give you a really hard time and make you feel angry. Thank goodness for my mentor's good advice not to respond immediately.

Exercise

The next time someone angers you while networking:

1. Wait. See if someone will chime in with a positive response. If no one is available, wait to respond. I did not immediately respond to the HR organization and Jamie via e-mail because it might have sounded defensive.

2. Step back. Stop interacting with the connections who make you angry until you cool off. Although I felt really angry and betrayed by my business mentor, I went for a walk, then caught up on other e-mails.

3. Seek to understand. Can e-mails be misinterpreted? Of course! Not only can you misinterpret e-mails but also others can misinterpret yours. Prior to responding to Jamie, I wrote an e-mail about how I did not appreciate how she "threw me under the bus." Then I thought, *Would I want to read any part of this on the front page of the newspaper? Would I be embarrassed if others read it?* Since the answer to both of those questions was yes, I threw it away and started over with a more positive tone, then picked up the phone.

NETWORKING DIARY PRINCIPLE 7

NETWORKING OPPORTUNITIES ARE EVERYWHERE

Learn to listen. Opportunity could be knocking at your door very softly. –Frank Tyger

"Networking" can seem like a trendy buzzword, but it's important to remember that it's just a simple conversation that can take place anywhere—the gas station, a buffet line, a wedding reception, and even a four-year-old's birthday party. I tell my employees, "You can't build your brand or clientele in a box." Meaning, "If your goal is to expand your network or sell your brand, never miss an opportunity to chat with others." Today, a client called our salon for an appointment, and I asked her whether she'd heard about us. She said that one of my employees gave her a business card at a nearby electronics store and that she was excited to get her hair cut with us. Every time my employees leave our salon for a break, I yell out, "Make sure to make friends!" It's the code for, "Introduce yourself to potential customers!" Try to feel comfortable chatting with people even if you have a job, because business is based on meaningful connections—and you can't build relationships sitting in silence.

Networking Diary Entry
December 7

While sitting at my work desk during lunchtime, I saw a nice man pay for a *USA Today* at a newspaper machine outside the door. I smiled and waved hello—what Southerners naturally do. The man entered my store to shake my hand and I said, "Hi and welcome! It is a pleasure to meet you. Please come back anytime for your next haircut." He enthusiastically replied, "Great thanks! Here is my card." His card read:

North Carolina

Department of Human Service

Division of Public Health

Glenn A. Ruess, PHR

5605 Six Forks Rd.

Raleigh, NC 27699-1930

I immediately asked this new contact, "You work in Human Resources?"

"Yes I do. I work for the State," he replied.

"I used to work in Human Resources for the City of Chicago," I said. "We should exchange notes about our HR experiences. I'd love to pick your brain sometime. How about we connect through LinkedIn?"

"Sounds good," he said. "I will send you an invitation through e-mail to connect."

Glenn left to go back to his human resources office and e-mailed me the same day to connect through LinkedIn.

Moving to a new city is emotionally and professionally challenging. Glenn was the first professional with whom I would be having a networking brunch since moving from Chicago to Raleigh. It is tough when you feel as though everyone already has their circle of friends and professional contacts. It can be especially difficult in a suburban environment to network as a single professional without children. Sometimes, I feel as though professionals with children tend to network with other parents. However, I could be wrong. It was just going to take some time to understand how people network with new professionals in the area who are single and without children.

Here are our e-mail exchanges up until our networking breakfast:

To: Glenn Ruess, PHR
From: Nancy T. Nguyen, MBA
Date: December 7
Re: Join my network on LinkedIn

Hello Glenn,

Thank you for your e-mail. It was a pleasure to meet you. I am headed to Chicago on Friday and will be back on Monday. Mornings are good. My store opens at 10 a.m., so if you know of anywhere where professionals meet for breakfast, it'd be great to meet. Let me know what you think.

Nancy

To: Nancy T. Nguyen, MBA
From: Glenn Ruess, PHR
Date: December 7
Re: Join my network on LinkedIn

Hello Nancy,

LOL, where professionals meet for breakfast—that's a good question! Ever eaten @ Courtney's, which is actually pretty close to your salon on Six Forks. I think they serve breakfast. I'll check to make sure if it's a place you'd like to go? Panera's another option.

Chicago, huh? Well I hope you have a nice, safe trip - to & back!

Glenn

To: Glenn Ruess, PHR
From: Nancy T. Nguyen, MBA
Date: December 7
Re: Join my network on LinkedIn

Glenn,

I love Courtney's! What I like to do is park at the store and walk over. That works. Want to shoot for Tuesday (12/14) morning at 9:00 a.m.?

Nancy

To: Nancy T. Nguyen, MBA
From: Glenn Ruess, PHR
Date: December 7
Re: Join my network on LinkedIn

OK Nancy, well Courtney's it is then!

Glenn

To: Glenn Ruess, PHR
From: Nancy T. Nguyen, MBA
Date: December 7
Re: Join my network on LinkedIn

Sounds good! Let's touch base on Monday for a reminder.

Stay warm,
Nancy

To: Nancy T. Nguyen, MBA
From: Glenn Ruess, PHR
Date: December 13
Re: Join my network on LinkedIn

Hey Nancy, just touching base.
Hope you had a great weekend up in Chicago! Was thinking about you up there while watching some of the Bears/Patriots game yesterday with all the snow—holy cow that looked cold!

Does 9 a.m. @ Courtney's still work for you on Tuesday?

Glenn

To: Glenn Ruess, PHR
From: Nancy T. Nguyen, MBA
Date: December 13
Re: Join my network on LinkedIn

Sounds good. I will get there probably around 9:05 because I am parking at the salon and walking over.

After this e-mail, Glenn offered to meet me at my store and drive me over. I thought, *Is this man crazy? I don't even know him!* However, I sent an e-mail that said, "That is so sweet. I will walk over. The cold air will feel good :)."

The morning of our meeting, it felt like a Chicago winter, with the cold, crisp air. The temperature in Raleigh is actually 15 degrees *lower* than it is in Chicago. It was nice to bundle up in layers, hat, and gloves and walk to our breakfast. I was looking forward to chatting about our careers in Human Resources.

My right foot stepped off the sidewalk, and the next thing I knew, I was lying down in the middle of morning rush hour traffic. Before the traffic light turned green, I got up and thought, *Oh my gosh! I've just been hit by an SUV!*

My right hand clutched my left shoulder where the point of impact had been. I moved my left arm in a full circle to make sure my arm was functioning. All of a sudden, I heard the driver of the SUV that hit me yell out of his window, "What happened?" A woman yelled back, "You just *hit* a little girl!" The driver sped off. I continued to walk across the street to the breakfast destination to tell Glenn that there would be a change of plans for our networking breakfast—to say the least.

The pain of the SUV striking my left shoulder and throwing me to the cold ground numbed my thoughts while strangers asked me questions. I could hear, "Are you okay?" "Do you need an ambulance?" "What is your name?" but no words could escape my mouth. All I could think was, *I just purchased a hair salon, moved back to Raleigh, and we do not have enough staff for the upcoming holiday rush. What if I can never use my left arm again?!"*

By this time, Glenn tried to ask questions, too. He asked what I wanted to do, and thoughts of hunger, pain, embarrassment, fear, and concern crossed my mind. Glenn offered again to drive me—only this time to the emergency room. Finally, I said, "Can we please go to my salon to cancel my first client's appointment?"

After calling my client, the pain in my left shoulder and knees began to take my breath away. I returned to Glenn's car and allowed this complete stranger to drive me to the Duke emergency room.

Glenn dropped me off at the Emergency Room entrance, and I walked up to the receptionist's desk with a smile and said, "Hi, I'm Nancy, and was just hit by an SUV on Six Forks Road."

The woman's countenance read, *You what? You don't look like you've been hit by an SUV.* I repeated, "Yes ma'am, a man's truck hit me, and I need x-rays." Surprisingly, Glenn showed up to guide me to the emergency room registration desk. At this point, my pride was wounded. Not only had this networking breakfast moved to the emergency room but also my left shoulder felt broken. My lips quivered when I said, "I apologize for taking up so much of your time." Glenn assured me that everything was going to be okay.

This stranger was kind enough to stay with me in the emergency room. The nurse helped me remove all of my clothes in exchange for a hospital gown. My poor networking buddy stood frozen in the corner. At this point, I did not care about my dignity since the pain had spread throughout my entire body.

While waiting on the hospital bed, a police officer arrived and began to question me regarding the accident so that he could write a report. This was a great networking opportunity!

Despite all the pain, fear, and confusion, I asked the police officer several questions about himself. He shared that he was from Poughkeepsie, NY, residing in Raleigh, and then told me a little about his family. This is networking! It is simply a conversation. Earlier in the book, I mention that "networking" is a buzzword, but it is simply a conversation about the other person. Your goal as a networker is to learn about the other person, find out what their needs are, and try to find a way to help the person or find something in common with him or her.

Before the officer left, I told him, "I actually went to a wedding in Poughkeepsie, NY a couple of months ago." We talked a bit more about New York and exchanged cards.

A nurse brought me fuzzy blue socks with slip-proof rubber on the bottom and asked me to follow her to the x-ray room. I grabbed a few business cards from my bag and headed toward the x-ray room. My body began to shake uncontrollably when the x-ray technician asked, "You were hit by an SUV while walking?"

"Yes ma'am, I was," I replied. "My salon is across the street, and I was trying to be green and walk to breakfast. The driver and I did not see each other, but he left the scene of the accident."

"This is crazy! You have a salon across the street?" the technician asked.

This was another networking opportunity! I invited her or anyone else who could use our services to come to the shop. Granted, most people would not have business cards on them while getting x-rays after being hit by an SUV. However, even in this situation, I saw the opportunity to apply all seven networking principles.

I walked back to my hospital bed and saw that my networking buddy was still standing in the corner waiting.

"Maybe it is time that you have a seat and relax," I told him. "Again, I truly apologize for taking up your time this morning." We continued to chat about our families and careers and discovered that we both once lived in the Midwest.

The doctor interrupted us by saying, "You broke it!"

Broke WHAT? I thought. He pointed on the x-ray to where my collarbone was broken. My heart began to drop because it was the holiday season, and my clients needed me to do their hair. Now I might not be able to work for weeks.

"Go to this orthopedic tomorrow, and they will tell you what to do," the doctor told me, handing me a slip of paper.

That's it? There is nothing that can take this pain away and fix everything right now? I thought. I also thought, *Tomorrow, there might be new people to meet at the orthopedic's office!*

An Asian nurse entered the room and dressed me as if I were a rag doll. I ended up in Glenn's car again. He drove me to my store. We decided to redo our networking breakfast in a few weeks. Since that day, Glenn and I have referred employees and valuable clients to each other.

DIARY ENTRY LEARNING LESSONS

When people hear about me being hit by an SUV, then networking in the emergency room, I hear, "You are crazy!" Whether you think I am crazy or not, the point is that there are always opportunities to network. The next time you are at a gas station, grocery store, or airport, look for opportunities to network with a purpose.

1. Starting a conversation is nerve-wracking at times. I simply say, "Hi, I'm Nancy. It is nice to meet you." It works every time, coupled with a good handshake and a smile. More than likely, the other person will respond and you can ask a few basic questions about them.

2. Remember to network with a purpose. You don't want to waste your time by talking to everyone. I happened to talk to everyone at the hospital across the street from my salon because everyone knows someone who could use a haircut. Think about the purpose of your conversation. Is it simply to find out who they are? Is it to share information?

3. Find out what that person's purpose is. Find out his or her story. Where does he or she work? What groups does he or she belong to? Is there any potential for you to help the person? Try to find a way to offer the person information or a resource to help him or her.

EXERCISE

The next time you are out in public, think:

1. Where are there potential and purposeful networking opportunities?

2. What can I do to help the person with whom I am connecting?

Take the time to identify potential networking opportunities, then think about how you can help the contact.

PART III – READY, SET, NETWORK

NETWORKING IN THE (BAD) BOY'S CLUB

Supposedly, women face different opportunities and challenges in the workplace and in networking. I had never even heard of the terms "the glass ceiling" and "sexual harassment" until my late 20s. Maybe it is a good thing that these terms are a bit foreign to me. Or maybe women have come a long way in the business world. Many generations of the "good ol' boy" network consist of helping young men along their career paths. As an Asian American gal who was bred in the South, the "boy's club" never bothered me. My dad is a diesel mechanic, so I've always enjoyed hanging out with his clients, talking sports and money. As a professional hairstylist, I served many members of the "boy's club." As a big Pittsburgh Steelers, Chicago White Sox, and NC State Wolfpack fan, there is usually always something to bring up with "the boys."

The following is an example of two boys who were not so "good ol' boys."

RUN, SCREAM, OR IGNORE?

February 20
Re: Great to run into you

Nick,

It was a pleasure to meet you at the prospective member orientation today. The information that you gave me was very helpful. I have recently joined the Yahoo! group that you mentioned.

After the meeting, I was offered the HR Assistant position at the White Sox field! I begin my MBA HR internship position on Monday. Once I adapt to my new schedule, I look forward to joining the HR organization and meeting other members like you.

Stay in touch!

Best regards,
Nancy

February 20
Re: Great to run into you

Hi Nancy:

First off . . . please call me Nick, OK? I'm glad you're already connected with the HR Transition . . . and when it's time for you to get more active in the search, I'd strongly advise attending at least some of the meetings to build stronger relationships. Also, kudos to you on landing the position at Sox Park . . . er . . . uh . . . I mean US Cellular Field.

Yeah . . . I'm somewhat old school in that I don't care for the corporate monikers that so many stadiums have these days! :)

I'll certainly keep in touch, and if there's any way I can be of assistance, please let me know.

Best regards,
Nick

August 29
Re: Great to run into you (again)

Nick,

It was great running into you again recently! I told my boss, and she was really excited that we went to the roundtable.

I look forward to seeing you at a future event. In the meantime, if you know of any HR internship positions open, I am looking for one to apply to. Have a wonderful day!

Best regards,
Nancy

August 29
Re: Great to run into you (again)

Hi Nancy:

You beat me to the punch! Indeed, I enjoyed reconnecting with you at the most recent roundtable after our initial meet at the LinkedIn session. I really like your personal style and level of energy! In regards to your internship, is there a particular time period that you are looking for? I'm guessing your program calls for two internship "tours of duty" given that you are currently doing one with your boss? Also, is there a particular hourly rate you are seeking, or is this an unpaid position?

Let's stay connected!

Best regards,
Nick

Although Nick was twice my age, for months, we crossed paths and provided each other with contacts, articles, and resources. When I landed a new HR job, I found out that my new boss was also connected to Nick. The HR circle is so small! We went out on a business meeting with Nick to talk about my new and exciting HR job.

I arrived to a nice place on Wacker Dr. in downtown Chicago, and Nick greeted me by the door in a suit and tie. He said, "Before we walk in for dinner . . ." He then paused to land a kiss on my lips before adding, " . . . this is something that I always wanted to do."

Ugh, gross!

Yes, I should have screamed, cried, or run away. He had been a very good friend and a HUGE HR contact in the City of Chicago, in addition to being friends with my current and former bosses. Stunned and speechless, I completely ignored his random kiss, like skipping the commercial part of a show using Tivo.

If that happened today, I would probably have a much different reaction. I would have directly said, "This is not appropriate at all since we are having a business meeting."

Remember that touching someone else's body or making comments that are sexual in any way are always inappropriate behaviors both in and out of the workplace. If you receive uninvited touching or sexual comments, leave the situation or remind the person that you are on a business meeting.

Sometimes, it is hard to make it so that networking does not appear as flirting. When a woman pays attention to a man by asking him questions about himself, many men see this as an invitation or believe that the woman may be interested in him. The best way I have found to handle this situation is to include the following statement in meeting confirmation e-mails: "I look forward to our business meeting." Then, when I arrive at the meeting, I extend a firm handshake. But as a young professional starting out, I really did not know how to respond to having a mentor land a random kiss on me.

TELL, TEXT, OR IGNORE?

 May 13
Re: Missed class, can you help?

Hi Nancy,

I just tried calling you. I had a meeting run over this morning, and it has thrown my whole day off. I am not sure I can make it to campus tonight. You indicated that you planned to be there. What time will you be available in case I can try to meet you this evening?

If not, can we meet before or after class on Thursday? I really appreciate your time here.

George

May 13
Re: Missed class, can you help?

George,

I hope that you have had a fantastic weekend.
Attached is the first half of notes for chapters 5-6.
Once I finish typing up the notes from class, it will be e-mailed. Accounting Problem # 2 is the only one that I can't get!
Problem 2 Part 1 - Interest Expense
I am still in the process of getting a few more notes to you.

Nancy

 May 13
Re: Missed class, can you help?

Nancy,

Thank you very much. I believe it's 510000 and 540000 because they used 20 payments rather than 40.
Thanks and have a good weekend!

George

George is another respected HR guy from school. He is a little league dad and was a great classmate. One night, he accidentally drunk texted me and said, "If only I was younger and not married . . ."

The next morning, he sent me a string of apology texts. He was mortified the next day in class and is still embarrassed to see me, but I have just learned to gracefully exit uncomfortable situations and not embarrass the men involved. It's easy to talk about how creepy some business professionals are, but if you protect their reputation, it will strengthen *your* reputation.

DIARY ENTRY LEARNING LESSONS

Networking with the opposite sex is vital. Whether I have something in common with the "boys" or not, there is always an opportunity to make a positive impression and build a reputation as a professional while networking. I always meet in public and put my foot down if the networking situation is harmful or extremely inappropriate. Choosing to apply all seven Networking Diary Principles with anyone, including "bad boys," will lead to success in your networking endeavors.

Here are a few brief final notes regarding the lessons I have learned from my networking experiences. In short, your goals should be as follows:

1. Learn about the other person / find out who they are.

2. Find out what their needs are / what you have in common with them.

3. Try to find a way to help them / share information or a resource to get them further along.

Then the seven principles:

1. Make sure the relationship is mutually beneficial.

2. Define your networking goal.

3. Make sure you've clarified what you need out of the connection and what you're looking for from the other person.

4. Do not take for granted the time a contact provides to you; respond in turn and acknowledge what they are offering.

5. Building business relationships takes time. You are cultivating the contact. Don't forget to follow up.

6. Be professional even when someone else is not.

7. Connections can happen anywhere and everywhere. Meet people. Talk.

While I was serving as an Ambassador for DePaul Kellstadt Graduate School of Business and Executive Vice President of the DePaul MBA Association in Chicago, IL, many classmates asked me the following recurring questions that are not directly answered in my diary. I'd like to share the questions and my thoughts.

1. *"How do I start to network?"* — Start by defining your personal networking goal. Then check with your university, community calendars, or local professional groups for general networking opportunities.

2. *"I am shy! How can I overcome this and go networking?"* — Identify someone you know who is a master networker and ask if they will help you with introductions. If this person truly believes in your skill sets, they will be your advocate and help you make valuable connections.

3. *"How can I get a new job if I don't have time to network?"* — Today, there are many opportunities online. Virtual networking and recruiting events can be found at http://www.brazencareerist.com.

4. *"I have nothing to offer, so why should I go out and network?"* — If you have this attitude, you will never go out and determine whether this is the truth. Think hard about who you know and what skills you have and make a list. Everyone has *something* to offer.

5. *"What do I say when I network?"* — A lot of people have asked how to start off a conversation while networking. Why not try, "Hi, I'm (your name), we have not met." Then proceed to ask questions about why the person is there.

6. *"I don't understand networking. Can you help me?"* — Networking is simply creating synergy and meaningful relationships that you cultivate over time.

7. *"I don't have anyone to reach out to. Do you have suggestions?"* — With over 6 billion people in the world, there is someone for you. I suggest that you go back to defining your networking goal, then

reaching out to people who may be able to guide you towards that goal.

8. *"I really don't know what I want out of life. Whom do I talk to?"* — Think about what you might want to do. Talk to people who are already doing it and ask questions. I used to want to be an HR Executive at a Fortune 500 company. After interviewing several executives, I learned that it was not the best career path for me.

9. *"My job/education is not impressive, so why bother?"* — Remember when I told you that my father never even finished the 6th grade? Well, he's networking all the time because it builds his clientele and long-lasting friendships.

10. *"Should you follow up with every business card you receive, and if so, how?"* — Unless you find the relationship mutually beneficial, you don't have to. In fact, I have a stack of cards in my computer bag right now that I might not look at again.

11. *"Should you go to every networking event possible (casting a wide net) or focus on events in your industry?"* — Maybe at first you can cast a wide net to explore what is out there. Then you will find that you will run out of time and resources. When I first moved to a new city, started a new career path, or launched a new business, I tried to go to every interesting networking event. Now I only focus on young entrepreneur groups because I find the relationships in the groups mutually beneficial.

12. *"When is it appropriate to ask for a business card?"* — When you think that you will find it beneficial to connect later.

13. *"Is it appropriate to ask a senior level executive for a business card?"* — No, unless he or she asks for yours or asks for you to contact him or her.

14. *"When is it appropriate to send someone you meet your resume?"* — When they ask.

15. *"Is it appropriate to pass the business card of someone you met to someone else? For example, I meet you at an event; can I pass your information on to Tim?"* — If you ask for permission first.

16. *"A lot of affinity groups, Graduate Women in Business (GWB); National Association of Hispanic MBAs (NSHMBA), etc., have networking events. Is it appropriate to attend an event that is not your affinity group?"* — Of course! Although I am Asian American, I am an active member in the NC Hispanic Chamber of Commerce and have built relationships with many members. In fact, the executive board came on Mother's Day to my business' grand opening event. As long as you are respectful, professional, and using the networking principles I have shared, you will have networking success!

IF YOU'D LIKE TO LEARN MORE

Ali Brown
Visionary Mentor to Women Entrepreneurs, Philanthropist
CEO of Ali International, LLC
http://www.alibrown.com
Regarded as the voice for women's entrepreneurial success.

Mary Cantando
Growth Expert for Women Entrepreneurs
Owner, Speaker, Author
http://www.womansadvantage.biz/
*Engages audiences throughout the country with her insight
and understanding regarding the power and potential of
women business owners.*

Fabienne Frederickson
Founder of www.ClientAttraction.com
Creator of The Client Attraction System®
http://www.clientattraction.com
*Fabienne runs a 7-figure Client Attraction business teaching
solo-entrepreneurs worldwide how to attract more clients
and enjoy more freedom in their business.*

Ivan Misner
Founder, Chairman
BNI
http://ivanmisner.com/
Interacts with and trains the top ten percent of business networkers in the world. Called the "Father of Modern Networking" by CNN and the "Networking Guru," Dr. Misner is considered to be one of the world's leading experts on business networking.

Joel Whalen
Associate Professor/Academic Director of
Sales Leadership Program
DePaul University
http://joelwhalen.com/
Called The World's Foremost Authority on Business Communication, Dr. Whalen is a world-class educator who provides practical, research-based tools that apply to all professional communication.